THE CAMP FIRE GIRLS ON THE MARCH

or, Bessie King's Test of Friendship

JANE L. STEWART

1st WORLD
LIBRARY
Literary Society

The Camp Fire Girls on the March

Jane L. Stewart

© 1st World Library, 2007
PO Box 2211
Fairfield, IA 52556
www.1stworldlibrary.com
First Edition

LCCN: 2007930799

Softcover ISBN: 978-1-4218-4842-6
Hardcover ISBN: 978-1-4218-4745-0
eBook ISBN: 978-1-4218-4939-3

Purchase *"The Camp Fire Girls on the March"*
as a traditional bound book at:
www.1stWorldLibrary.com/purchase.asp?ISBN=978-1-4218-4842-6

1st World Library is a literary, educational organization
dedicated to:

- Creating a free internet library of downloadable ebooks

- Hosting writing competitions and offering book publishing
scholarships.

Interested in more 1st World Library books? contact:
literacy@1stworldlibrary.com
Check us out at: www.1stworldlibrary.com

1st World Library Literary Society

Giving Back to the World

"If you want to work on the core problem, it's early school literacy."

- James Barksdale, former CEO of Netscape

"No skill is more crucial to the future of a child, or to a democratic and prosperous society, than literacy."

- Los Angeles Times

"Literacy... means far more than learning how to read and write... The aim is to transmit... knowledge and promote social participation."

- UNESCO

"Literacy is not a luxury, it is a right and a responsibility. If our world is to meet the challenges of the twenty-first century we must harness the energy and creativity of all our citizens."

- President Bill Clinton

"Parents should be encouraged to read to their children, and teachers should be equipped with all available techniques for teaching literacy, so the varying needs and capacities of individual kids can be taken into account."

- Hugh Mackay

CHAPTER I

AN UNEXPECTED VISITOR

"Oh, what a glorious day!" cried Bessie King, the first of the members of the Manasquan Camp Fire Girls of America to emerge from the sleeping house of Camp Sunset, on Lake Dean, and to see the sun sparkling on the water of the lake. She was not long alone in her enjoyment of the scene, however.

"Oh, it's lovely!" said Dolly Ransom, as, rubbing her eyes sleepily, since it was only a little after six, she joined her friend on the porch. "This is really the first time we've had a chance to see what the lake looks like. It's been covered with that dense smoke ever since we've been here."

"Well, the smoke has nearly all gone, Dolly. The change in the wind not only helped to put out the fire, but it's driving the smoke away from us."

"The smoke isn't all gone, though, Bessie. Look over there. It's still rising from the other end of the woods on the other side of the lake, but it isn't bothering us over here any more."

"What a pity it is that we've got to go away just as the weather gives us a chance to enjoy it here! But then I guess we'll have a good time when we do go away, anyhow. We thought we weren't going to enjoy it here, but it hasn't been so bad, after all, has it?"

"No, because it ended well, Bessie. But if those girls in the camp next door had had their way, we wouldn't have had a single pleasant thing to remember about staying here, would we?"

"They've had their lesson, I think, Dolly. Perhaps they won't be so ready to look down on the Camp Fire Girls after this— and I'm sure they would be nice and friendly if we stayed."

"I wouldn't want any of their friendliness. All I'd ask would be for them to let us alone. That's all I ever did want them to do, anyhow. If they had just minded their own affairs, there wouldn't have been any trouble."

"Well, I feel sort of sorry for them, Dolly. When they finally got into real trouble they had to come to us for help, and if they are the sort of girls they seem to be, they couldn't have liked doing that very well."

"You bet they didn't, Bessie! It was just the hardest thing they could have done. You see, the reason they were so mean to us is that they are awfully proud, and they think they're better than any other people."

"Then what's the use of still being angry at them? I thought you weren't last night—not at Gladys Cooper, at least."

"Why, I thought then that she was in danger because of what I'd done, and that made me feel bad. But you and I helped to get her back to their camp safely, so I feel as if we were square. I suppose I ought to be willing to forgive them for the way they acted, but I just can't seem to do it, Bessie."

Jane L. Stewart

"Well, as long as we're going away from here to-day any-how, it doesn't make much difference. We're not likely to see them again, are we?"

"I don't know why not—those who live in the same town, anyhow. Marcia Bates and Gladys Cooper—the two who were lost on the mountain last night, you know—live very close to me at home."

"You were always good friends with Gladys until you met her up here, weren't you?"

"Oh, yes, good friends enough. I don't think we either of us cared particularly about the other. Each of us had a lot of friends we liked better, but we got along well enough."

"Well, don't you think she just made a mistake, and then was afraid to admit it, and try to make up for it? I think lots of people are like that. They do something wrong, and then, just because it frightens them a little and they think it would be hard to set matters right, they make a bad thing much worse."

"Oh, you can't make me feel charitable about them, and there's no use trying, Bessie! Let's try not to talk about them, for it makes me angry every time I think of the way they behaved. They were just plain snobs, that's all!"

"I thought Gladys Cooper was pretty mean, after all the trouble we had taken last night to help her and her chum, but I do think the rest were sorry, and felt that they'd been all wrong. They really said so, if you remember."

"Well, they ought to have been, certainly! What a lot of lazy girls they must be! Do look, Bessie. There isn't a sign of life over at their camp. I bet not one of them is up yet!"

"You're a fine one to criticise anyone else for being lazy, Dolly Ransom! How long did it take me to wake you up this morning? And how many times have you nearly missed breakfast by going back to bed after you'd pretended to get up?"

"Oh, well," said Dolly, defiantly, "it's just because I'm lazy myself and know what a fault it is that I'm the proper one to call other people down for it. It's always the one who knows all about some sin who can preach the best sermon against it, you know."

"Turning preacher, Dolly?" asked Eleanor Mercer. Both the girls spun around and rushed toward her as soon as they heard her voice, and realized that she had stepped noiselessly out on the porch. They embraced her happily. She was Guardian of the Camp Fire, and no more popular Guardian could have been found in the whole State.

"Dolly's got something more against the girls from Halsted Camp!" explained Bessie, with a peal of laughter. "She says they're lazy because they're not up yet, and I said she was a fine one to say anything about that! Don't you think so too, Miss Eleanor?"

"Well, she's up early enough this morning, Bessie. But, well, I'm afraid you're right. Dolly's got a lot of good qualities, but getting up early in the morning unless someone pulls her out of bed and keeps her from climbing in again, isn't one of them."

"What time are we going to start, Miss Eleanor?" asked Dolly, who felt that it was time to change the topic of conversation. Dolly was usually willing enough to talk about herself, but she preferred to choose the subject herself.

Jane L. Stewart

"After we've had breakfast and cleaned things up here. It was very nice of the Worcesters to let us use their camp, and we must leave it looking just as nice as when we came."

"Are they coming back here this summer?"

"The Worcesters? No, I don't think so. I'm pretty sure, though, that they have invited some friends of theirs to use the camp next week and stay as long as they like."

"I hope their friends will please the Halsted Camp crowd better than we did," said Dolly, sarcastically. "The Worcesters ought to be very careful only to let people come here who are a little better socially than those girls. Then they'd probably be satisfied."

"Now, don't hold a grudge against all those girls, Dolly," said Eleanor, smiling. "Gladys Cooper was really the ringleader in all the trouble they tried to make for us, and you've had your revenge on her. On all of them, for that matter."

"Oh, Miss Eleanor, if you could only have seen them when I threw that basket full of mice among them! I never saw such a scared lot of girls in my life!"

"That was a pretty mean trick," said Eleanor. "I don't think what they did to bother us deserved such a revenge as that, even if I believed in revenge, anyhow. I don't because it usually hurts the people who get it more than the victims."

Bessie looked at Dolly sharply, but, if she meant to say anything, Eleanor herself anticipated her remark.

"Now come on, Dolly, own up!" she said. "Didn't you feel pretty bad when you heard Gladys and Marcia were lost in the woods last night? Didn't you think that it was because you'd got the best of the girls that they turned against Gladys, and so drove her into taking that foolish night walk in the woods?"

"Oh, I did—I did!" cried Dolly. "And I told Bessie so last night, too. I never would have forgiven myself if anything really serious had happened to those two girls."

"That's just it, Dolly. You may think that revenge is a joke, perhaps, as you meant yours to be, but you never can tell how far it's going, nor what the final effect is going to be."

"I'm beginning to see that, Miss Mercer."

"I know you are, Dolly. You were lucky—as lucky as Gladys and Marcia. You were particularly lucky, because, after all, it was your pluck in going into that cave, when you didn't know what sort of danger you might run into, that found them. So you had a salve for your conscience right then. But often and often it wouldn't have happened that way. You might very well have had to remember always that your revenge, though you thought it was such a trifling thing, had had a whole lot of pretty serious results."

"Well, I really am beginning to feel a little sorry," admitted Dolly, "though Gladys acted just as if she was insulted because we found them. She said she and Marcia would have been all right in that cave if they'd stayed there until morning."

"I think she'll have reason to change her mind," said Eleanor. "She'd have found herself pretty uncomfortable this morning with nothing to eat. And she's in for a bad cold, unless I'm mistaken, and it might very well have been pneumonia if they'd had to stay out all night."

"She's a softy!" declared Dolly, scornfully. "I'll bet Bessie and I could have spent the night there and been all right, too, after it was all over."

"You and Bessie are both unusually strong and healthy, Dolly. It may not be her fault that she's a softy, as you call her. The Camp Fire pays a whole lot of attention to health. That's why Health is one of the words that we use to make up Wo-he-lo. Work, and Health, and Love. Because you can't work properly, and love properly, unless you are healthy."

"I suppose what happened to Gladys last night was one of the things you were talking about when you wanted us to be patient, wasn't it?"

"What do you mean, Dolly?"

"Why, when you said that pride went before a fall, and that she'd be sure to have something unpleasant happen if we only let her alone, and didn't try to get even ourselves?"

"Well, it looks like it, doesn't it?"

"I don't get much satisfaction out of seeing people punished that way, though," admitted Dolly, after a moment's thought. "It seems to me—well, listen, Miss Eleanor. Suppose some-one did something awfully nice for me. It wouldn't be right, would it, for me just to say to myself, 'Oh, well, something nice will happen to her.' She might have some piece of good fortune, but I wouldn't have anything to do with it. I'd want to do something nice myself to show that I was grateful."

"Of course you would," said Eleanor, who saw the point Dolly was trying to make and admired her power of working out a logical proposition.

"Well, then, if that's true, why shouldn't it be true if someone does something hateful to me? I don't take any credit for the pleasant things that happen to people who are nice to me, so why should I feel satisfied because the hateful ones have some piece of bad luck that I didn't have anything to do with, either?"

"That's a perfectly good argument as far as it goes, Dolly. But the trouble is that it doesn't go far enough. You've got a false step in it. Can't you see where she goes wrong, Bessie?"

"I think I can, Miss Eleanor," said Bessie. "It's that we ought not to be glad when people are in trouble, even if they are mean to us, isn't it? But we are glad, and ought to be, when nice people have good luck. So the two cases aren't the same a bit, are they?"

"Right!" said Eleanor, heartily. "Think that over a bit, Dolly. You'll see the point pretty soon and then maybe you'll understand the whole business better."

Just then the girls whose turn it had been to prepare breakfast came to the door of the Living Camp, which contained the dining-room and the kitchen, and a blast on a horn announced that breakfast was ready.

"Come on! We'll eat our next meal sitting around a camp fire in the woods, if that forest fire has left any woods where we're going," announced Eleanor. "So we want to make this meal a good one. No telling what sort of places we'll find on our tramp."

"I bet it will be good fun, no matter what they're like," said Margery Burton, one of the other members of the Camp Fire. She was a Fire-Maker, the second rank of the Camp Fire. First are the Wood-Gatherers, to which Bessie and Dolly belonged; then the Fire-Makers, and finally, and next to the Guardian, whom they serve as assistants, the Torch-Bearers. Margery hoped soon to be made a Torch-Bearer, and had an ambition to become a Guardian herself as soon as Miss Eleanor and the local council of the National Camp Fire decided that she was qualified for the work.

"Oh, you'd like any old thing just because you had to stand for it, Margery, whether it was any good or not," said Dolly.

"Well, isn't that a good idea? Why, I even manage to get along with you, Dolly! Sometimes I like you quite well. And anyone who could stand for you!"

Dolly laughed as loudly as the rest. She had been pretty thoroughly spoiled, but her association with the other girls in the Camp Fire had taught her to take a joke when it was aimed at her, unlike most people who are fond of making jokes at the expense of others, and of teasing them. She recognized that she had fairly invited Margery's sharp reply.

"We'll have to hurry and get ready when breakfast is over," said Eleanor as they were finishing the meal. "You girls whose turn it is to wash up had better get through as quickly as you can. Then we'll all get the packs ready. We have to take the boat that leaves at half past nine for the other end of Lake Dean."

"Why, there's someone coming! It's those girls from the other camp!" announced Dolly, suddenly. She had left the table, and was looking out of the window.

And, sure enough, when the Camp Fire Girls went out on the porch in a minute, they saw advancing the private school girls, whose snobbishness had nearly ruined their stay at Camp Sunset. Marcia Bates, who had been rescued with her friend, Gladys Cooper, acted as spokesman for them.

"We've come to tell you that we've all decided we were nasty and acted like horrid snobs," she said. "We have found out that you're nice girls—nicer than we are. And we're very grateful—of course I am, especially—for you helping us. And so we want you to accept these little presents we've brought for you."

CHAPTER II

TROUBLE SMOOTHED AWAY

Probably none of the Camp Fire Girls had ever been so surprised in their lives as when they heard the object of this utterly unexpected visit. Marcia's eyes were rather blurred while she was speaking, and anyone could see that it was a hard task she had assumed.

It is never easy to confess that one has been in the wrong, and it was particularly hard for these girls, whose whole campaign against the Camp Fire party had been based on pride and a false sense of their own superiority, which, of course, had existed only in their imaginations.

For a moment no one seemed to know what to do or say. Strangely enough, it was Dolly, who had resented the previous attitude of the rich girls more than any of her companions, who found by instinct the true solution.

She didn't say a word; she simply ran forward impulsively and threw her arms about Marcia's neck. Then, and not till then, as she kissed the friend with whom she had quarreled, did she find words.

"You're an old dear, Marcia!" she cried. "I knew you

wouldn't keep on hating us when you knew us better—and you'll forgive me, won't you, for playing that horrid trick with the mice?"

Dolly had broken the ice, and in a moment the stiffness of the two groups of girls was gone, and they mingled, talking and laughing naturally.

"I don't know what the presents you brought are—you haven't shown them to us yet," said Dolly, with a laugh. "But I'm sure they must be lovely, and as for accepting them, why, you just bet we will!"

"You know," said Marcia a little apologetically, "there aren't any real stores up here, and we couldn't get what we would really have liked, but we just did the best we could. Girls, get those things out!"

And then a dozen blankets were unrolled, beautifully woven Indian blankets, such as girls love to use for their dens, as couch covers and for hangings on the walls. Dolly exclaimed with delight as she saw hers.

"Heavens! And you act as if they weren't perfectly lovely!" she cried. "Why, Marcia, how can you talk as if they weren't the prettiest things! If that's what you call just doing the best you can, I'm afraid to think of what you'd have got for us if you'd been able to pick out whatever you wanted. It would have been something so fine that we'd have been afraid to take it, I'm sure."

"Well, we thought perhaps you'd find them useful if you're going on this tramp of yours," said Marcia, blushing with pleasure. "And I'm ever so glad you like them, if you really do, because I helped to pick them out. There's one for each of you, and then we've got a big Mackinaw jacket for Miss

Mercer, so that she'd have something different."

"I can't tell you how happy this makes me!" said Eleanor, swallowing a little hard, for she was evidently deeply touched. "I don't mean the presents, Marcia, though they're lovely, but the spirit in which you all bring them."

"We—we wanted to show you we were sorry, and that we understood how mean we'd been," said Marcia.

"Oh, my dear, do let's forget all that!" said Eleanor, heartily. "We don't want to remember anything unpleasant. Let's bury all that, and just have the memory that we're all good friends now, and that we'd never have been anything else if we'd only understood one another in the beginning as well as we do now.

"That's the reason for most of the quarrels in this world; people don't understand one another, that's all. And when they do, it's just as it is with us—they wonder how they ever could have hated one another!"

"Why, where's Gladys Cooper?" asked Dolly, suddenly. She had been looking around for the girl who had been chiefly responsible for all the trouble, and who had been, before this meeting, one of Dolly's friends in the city from which she and Marcia, as well as the Camp Fire Girls, came. And Gladys was missing.

"She—why—she—she isn't feeling very well," stammered Marcia unhappily. But a look at Dolly's face convinced her that she might as well tell the truth. "I'm awfully sorry," she went on shamefacedly, "but Gladys was awfully silly."

"You mean she hasn't forgiven us?" said Eleanor gently.

"She's just stupid," flashed Marcia. "What has she got to forgive? She ought to be here, thanking Dolly and Bessie King for finding us, just as I am. And she's sulking in her room, instead!"

"She'll change her mind, Marcia," said Eleanor, "just as the rest of you have done. I'm dreadfully sorry that she feels that way, because it must make her unhappy. But please don't be angry with her if you really want to please us. We're just as ready and just as anxious to be friends with her as with all the rest of you, and some time we will be, too. I'm sure of that."

"We'll make her see what a fool she is!" said Marcia, hotly. "If she'd only come with us, she'd have seen it for herself. She said all the girls here would crow over us, and act as if we were backing down, and had done this because someone made us."

Eleanor laughed heartily.

"Well, that is a silly idea!" she said. "Just explain to her that we were just as pleased and as surprised to see you as we could be, Marcia. You didn't need to come here this way at all, and we know it perfectly well. You did it just because you are nice girls and wanted to be friendly, and we appreciate the way you've come a good deal more than we do the lovely presents, even."

"Well, I hope we'll see you again," said Marcia. "If you're going on that half past nine boat we'll go back now, and let you pack, unless we can help you?"

"No, you can't help us. We've really got very little to do. But don't go. Stay around, if you will, and we'll all talk and visit with you while we do what there is to be done."

"I'm awfully sorry Gladys is cutting up so. It makes me feel ashamed, Dolly," said Marcia, when she and Dolly were alone. "But you know how she is. I think she's really just as sorry as the rest of us, but—"

"But she's awfully proud, and she won't show it, Marcia. I know, for I'm that way myself, though I really do think I've been behaving myself a little better since I've belonged to the Camp Fire. I wish you'd join, Marcia."

"Maybe I will, Dolly."

"Oh, that would be fine! Shall I speak to Miss Eleanor? She'd be perfectly delighted, I know."

"No, don't speak to her yet. I've got a plan, or some of us have, rather, but it's still a secret so I can't tell you anything about it. But maybe I'll have a great surprise for you the next time I see you."

The time passed quickly and pleasantly, and all too soon Miss Eleanor had to give the word that it was time to start for the landing if they were to catch the little steamer that was to take them to the other end of the lake.

"I tell you what! We'll all go with you as far as you go on the boat, and come back on her," said Marcia. "That will be good fun, won't it? I've got plenty of money for the fares, and those who haven't their money with them can pay me when we get back to camp."

All the girls from Camp Halsted fell in with her suggestion, delighted by the idea of such an unplanned excursion. It was easy enough to arrange it, too, for the little steamer would be back on her return trip early in the afternoon, even though she did not make very good speed and had numerous stops to make, since Lake Dean's shores were lined with little settlements, where camps and cottages and hotels, had been built at convenient spots.

"We've heard you singing a lot of songs we never heard before," said Marcia to Bessie, as they took their places on the boat. "Won't you teach us some of them? They were awfully pretty, we thought."

"You must mean the Camp Fire songs," said Bessie, happily. "We'll be glad to teach them to you—and they're all easy to learn, too. I think Dolly's got an extra copy of one of the song books and I know she'll be glad to let you have it."

And so, as soon as Bessie explained what Marcia wanted, the deck of the steamer was turned into an impromptu concert hall, and she made her journey to the strains of the favorite songs of the Camp Fire, the Wo-he-lo cheer with its lovely music being, of course, sung more often than any of the others.

"We were wondering so much about that," said Marcia. "We could make out the word Wo-he-lo, but we couldn't understand it. It sounded like an Indian word, but the others didn't seem to fit in with that idea."

"It's just made up from the first syllables of work and health and love, you see," said Eleanor. "We make up a lot of the words we use. A good many of the ceremonial names that the girls choose are made that way."

"Then they have a real meaning, haven't they?"

"Yes. You see, one of the things that we preach and try to teach in the Camp Fire is that things ought to be useful as well as beautiful. And it's very easy to be both."

Jane L. Stewart

"But tell me about the Indian sound of Wo-he-lo. Was that just an accident, or was it chosen that way on purpose?"

"Both, I think, Marcia. You see, the Indians in this country had a lot of good qualities that a great many people have forgotten or overlooked completely. Of course they were savages, in a way, but they had a civilization of their own, and a great many of their practices are particularly well adapted to this country."

"Oh, I see! You don't want them to be forgotten."

"That's just it. It's a good way to keep the memory of earlier times alive, and there seems to be something romantic and picturesque about the Indian names and the Indian things."

"That's one of the things I like best that I've found out about the Camp Fire since you came to Camp Sunset. We used to think the Camp Fire meant being goody-goody and learning to sew and cook and all sorts of things like that. But you have a lot of fun and good times, too, don't you?"

"Yes, and there really isn't anything goody-goody about us, Marcia. You'd soon find that out if you were with us."

"Well, I'm very glad that so many people have been led to know the truth about us," said Eleanor, with a smile. "If everyone knew the truth about the Camp Fire, it would soon be as big and as influential as even the most enthusiastic of us hope it will be. And I'm sure that we'll grow very fast now, because when girls understand us they see that we simply help them to have the sort of good times they enjoy most. Having a good time is a pretty important thing in this life."

"I—I rather thought you would think that we spent too much

time just having a good time," said Marcia, plainly rather surprised by this statement.

"I don't say anything about you girls in particular, because I don't know enough about you," replied Eleanor. "Of course, it's easy to get to be so bound up in enjoying yourself that you don't think of anything else. But people who do that soon get tired of just amusing themselves, so, as a rule, there's no great harm done. They get so that everything they do bores them, and they turn to something serious and useful, for a change."

"But you just said having a good time was important—"

"And I meant it," said Eleanor, with a smile. "Because it's just as bad to go to one extreme as to the other, and that's true in about everything. People who never work, but spend all their time playing aren't happy, as a rule, or healthy, either. And people who reverse that, and work all the time without ever playing, are in just about the same boat, only they're really worse off than the others, because it's harder for them to change."

"I think I'm beginning to see what you mean, Miss Mercer."

"Why, of course you are, Marcia! It's in the middle ground that the right answer lies. Work a little, and play a little, that's the way to get on and be happy. When you've worked hard, you need some sort of relaxation, and it's pretty important to know how to enjoy yourself, and have a good time."

"And you certainly can have bully good times in the Camp Fire," said Dolly, enthusiastically. "I've never enjoyed myself half so much as I have since I've belonged. Why, we have bacon bats, and picnics, and all sorts of things that are the best fun you ever dreamed of, Marcia. Much nicer than those stiff old parties you and I used to go to all the time, when we always did the same things, and could tell before we went just what was going to happen."

"And the regular camp fires, the ceremonial ones, Dolly," reminded Bessie. "Don't you think Marcia would enjoy that?"

"Oh, I know she would! Couldn't I bring her to one some time?" Dolly asked Eleanor.

"She'll be very welcome, any time," said Eleanor with a smile. "There's nothing secret about the Camp Fire meetings," she went on. "They're not a bit like high school and private school fraternities or sororities—whichever you call them."

"Why, look where we are!" said Marcia suddenly. "We'll be at the dock pretty soon."

"Why, so we will!" Eleanor said. "That's Cranford, sure enough, girls! We get off here, and begin our real tramp."

"I wish we were going with you," said Marcia, with a sigh of regret. "But we can't, of course. Well, I told Dolly we might have a surprise for her pretty soon, and we will if I've got anything to say about it, too. This has been awfully jolly! I guess I know a lot more about your Camp Fire now than I ever expected to. And I've enjoyed hearing every word, too."

Soon the little steamer was made fast to the dock, and the Camp Fire Girls streamed off, lining up on the dock. On the steamer the girls from Camp Halsted—all but Gladys Cooper, who had not made the trip—lined up, leaning over the rail.

"We'll see them off as the boat goes right back again," said Eleanor. "And let's give them the Wo-he-lo cheer for good-bye, girls."

So their voices rose on the quiet air as the steamer's whistle shrieked, and she began to pull out.

"Good-bye! Good luck!" cried Marcia and all the Halsted girls. "And come back whenever you can! We'll have a mighty different sort of welcome for you next time!"

"Good-bye! And thank you ever so much for the blankets!" called the Camp Fire Girls.

Jane L. Stewart

CHAPTER III

THE WORK OF THE FIRE

At Cranford began the road which the Camp Fire Girls were to follow through Indian Notch, the gap between the two big mountains, Mount Grant and Mount Sherman. Then they were to travel easily toward the seashore, since the Manasquan Camp Fire, ever since it had been organized, had spent a certain length of time each summer by the sea.

The Village of Cranford had been saved from the fire only by a shift of the wind. The woods to the west and the north had been burning briskly for several days, and every able-bodied man in the village had been out, day and night, with little food and less rest, trying to turn off the fire. In spite of all their efforts, however, they would have failed in their task if the change in the weather had not come to their aid. As a consequence, everyone in the village, naturally enough, was still talking about the fire.

"It isn't often that a village in this part of the country has such a narrow escape," said Eleanor, looking around, "See, girls, you can see for yourselves how close they were to having to turn and run from the fire."

"It looks as if some of the houses here had actually been on fire," said Dolly, as they passed into the outskirts of the village.

"I expect they were. You see, the wind was very high just before the shift came, and it would carry sparks and blazing branches. It's been a very hot, dry summer, too, and so all the wooden houses were ready to catch fire. The paint was dry and blistered. They probably had to watch these houses very carefully, to be ready to put out a fire the minute it started."

"It didn't look so bad from our side of the lake, though, did it?"

"The smoke hid the things that were really dangerous from us, but here they could see all right. I'll bet that before another summer comes around they'll be in a position to laugh at a fire."

"How do you mean? Is there anything they can do to protect themselves—before a fire starts, I mean?"

"That's the time to protect themselves. When people wait until the fire has actually begun to burn, it's almost impossible for them to check it. It would have been this time, if the wind had blown for a few hours longer the way it was doing when the fire started."

"But what can they do?"

"They can have a cleared space between the town and the forest, for one thing, with a lot of brush growing there, if they want to keep that. Then, if a fire starts, they can set the brush afire, and make a back fire, so that the big fire will be checked by the little one. The fire has to have something to feed on, you see, and if it comes to a cleared space that's fairly wide, it can't get any further.

Jane L. Stewart

"Oh, a cleared space like that doesn't mean that the village could go to sleep and feel safe! But it's a lot easier to fight the fire then. All the men in town could line up, with beaters and plenty of water, and as soon as sparks started a fire on their side of the clearing, they could put it out before it could get beyond control."

"Oh, I see! And being able to see the fire as soon as it started, they wouldn't have half so much trouble fighting it as if they had to be after the really big blaze."

"Yes. The fire problem in places like this seems very dreadful, but when the conditions are as good as they are here, with plenty of water, all that's needed is a little forethought. It's different in some of the lumber towns out west, because there the fires get such a terrific start that they would jump any sort of a clearing, and the only thing to do when a fire gets within a certain distance of a town is for the people who live in the town to run."

Soon the road began to pass between desolate stretches of woods, where the fire had raged at its hottest. Here the ground on each side of the road was covered with smoking ashes, and blackened stumps stood up from the barren, burnt ground.

"It looks like a big graveyard, with those stumps for head-stones," said Dolly, with a shudder.

"It is a little like that," said Eleanor, with a sigh. "But if you came here next year you wouldn't know the place. All that ash will fertilize the ground, and it will all be green. The stumps will still be there, but a great new growth will be beginning to push out. Of course it will be years and years before it's real forest again, but nature isn't dead, though it looks so. There's life underneath all that waste and desolation, and it will soon spring up again."

"I hope we'll get out of this burned country soon," said Dolly. "I think it's as gloomy and depressing as it can be. I'd like to have seen this road before the fire—it must have been beautiful."

"It certainly was, Dolly. And all this won't last for many miles. We really ought to stop pretty soon to eat our dinner. What do you say, girls? Would you like to wait, and press on until we come to a more cheerful spot, where the trees aren't all burnt!"

"Yes, oh, yes!" cried Margery Burton. "I think that would be ever so much nicer! Suppose we are a little hungry before we get our dinner? We can stand that for once."

"I think we'll enjoy our meal more. So we'll keep on, then, if the rest of you feel the same way."

Not a voice dissented from that proposition, either. Dolly was not the only one who was saddened by the picture of desolation through which they were passing. The road, of course, was deep in dust and ashes, and the air, still filled with the smoke that rose from the smouldering woods, was heavy and pungent, so that eyes were watery, and there was a good deal of coughing and sneezing.

"It's a lucky thing there weren't any houses along here, isn't it?" said Margery. "I don't see how they could possibly have been saved, do you, Miss Eleanor?"

"There's no way that they could have saved them, unless, perhaps, by having a lot of city fire engines, and keeping them completely covered with water on all sides while the fire was burning. They call that a water blanket, but of

Jane L. Stewart

course there's no way that they could manage that up here."

"What do you suppose started this fire, Miss Eleanor?"

"No one will ever know. Perhaps someone was walking in the woods, and threw a lighted cigar or cigarette in a pile of dry leaves. Perhaps some party of campers left their camp without being sure that their fire was out."

"Just think of it—that all the trouble could be started by a little thing like that! It makes you realize what a good thing it is that we have to be careful never to leave a single spark behind when we're leaving a fire, doesn't it?"

"Yes. It's a dreadful thing that people should be so careless with fire. Fire, and the heat we get from it, is responsible for the whole progress of the race. It was the discovery that fire could be used by man that was back of every invention that has ever been made."

"That's why it's the symbol of the Camp Fire, isn't it?"

"Yes. And in this country people ought to think more of fire than they do. We lose more by fire every year than any other country in the world, because we're so terribly careless."

"What is that there, ahead of us, in the road?" asked Bessie, suddenly. They had just come to a bend in the road, and about a hundred yards away a group of people stood in the road.

Eleanor looked grave. She shaded her eyes with her hand, and stared ahead of her.

"Oh," she cried, "what a shame! I remember now. There was a farm house there! I'm afraid we were wrong when we spoke of there being no houses in the path of this fire!"

They pressed on steadily, and, as they approached the group forlorn, distressed and unhappy, they saw that their fears were only too well grounded. The people in the road were staring, with drawn faces, at a scene of ruin and desolation that far outdid the burnt wastes beside the road, since what they were looking at represented human work and the toil of hands.

The foundations of a farm house were plainly to be seen, the cellar filled with the charred wood of the house itself, and in what had evidently been the yard there were heaps of ashes that showed where the barns and other buildings had stood.

In the road, staring dully at the girls as they came up, were two women and a boy about seventeen years old, as well as several young children.

Eleanor looked at them pityingly, and then spoke to the older of the two women.

"You seem to be in great trouble," she said. "Is this your house?"

"It was!" said the woman, bitterly. "You can see what's left of it! What are you—picnickers? Be off with you! Don't come around here gloating over the misfortunes of hard working people!"

"How can you think we'd do that?" said Eleanor, with tears in her eyes. "We can see that things look very bad for you. Have you any place to go—any home?"

"You can see it!" said the woman, ungraciously.

Eleanor looked at her and at the ruined farm for a minute very thoughtfully. Then she made up her mind.

"Well, if you've got to start all over again," she said, "you are going to need a lot of help, and I don't see why we can't be the first to help you! Girls, we won't go any further now. We'll stay here and help these poor people to get started!"

"What can people like you do to help us?" asked the woman, scornfully. "This isn't a joke—'t ain't like a quiltin' party!"

"Just you watch us, and see if we can't help," said Eleanor, sturdily. "We're not as useless as we look, I can tell you that! And the first thing we're going to do is to cook a fine dinner, and you are all going to sit right down on the ground and help us eat it. You'll be glad of a meal you don't have to cook yourselves, I'm sure. Where is your well, or your spring for drinking water? Show us that, and we'll do the rest!"

Only half convinced of Eleanor's really friendly intentions, the woman sullenly pointed out the well, and in a few moments Eleanor had set the girls to work.

"The poor things!" she said to Margery, sympathetically. "What they need most of all is courage to pick up again, now that everything seems to have come to an end for them, and make a new start. And I can't imagine anything harder than that!"

"Why, it's dreadful!" said Margery. "She seems to have lost all ambition—to be ready to let things go."

"That's just the worst of it," said Eleanor. "And it's in making them see that there's still hope and cheer and good friendship in the world that we can help them most. I do think we can be of some practical use to them, too, but the main thing is to brace them up, and make them want to be busy helping themselves. It would be so easy for me to give them the money to start over again or I could get my friends to come in with me, and make up the money, if I couldn't do it all myself."

"But they ought to do it for themselves, you mean?"

"Yes. They'll really be ever so much better off in the long run if it's managed that way. Often and often, in the city, I've heard the people who work in the charity organizations tell about families that were quite ruined because they were helped too much."

"I can see how that would be," said Margery. "They would get into the habit of thinking they couldn't do anything for themselves—that they could turn to someone else whenever they got into trouble."

"Yes. You see these poor people are in the most awful sort of trouble now. They're discouraged and hopeless. Well, the thing to do is to make them understand that they can rise superior to their troubles, that they can build a new home on the ashes of their old one."

"Oh, I think it will be splendid if we can help them to do that!"

"They'll feel better, physically, as soon as they have had a good dinner, Margery. Often and often people don't think enough about that. It's when people feel worst that they ought to be fed best. It's impossible to be cheerful on an empty stomach. When people are well nourished their troubles never seem so great. They look on the bright side and they tell themselves that maybe things aren't as bad as they look."

"How can we help them otherwise, though!"

"Oh, we'll fix up a place where they can sleep to-night, for one thing. And we'll help them to start clearing away all the rubbish. They've got to have a new house, of course, and they can't even start work on that until all this wreckage is cleared away."

"I wonder if they didn't save some of their animals—their cows and horses," said Bessie. "It seems to me they might have been able to do that."

"I hope so, Bessie. But we'll find out when we have dinner. I didn't want to bother them with a lot of questions at first. Look, they seem to be a little brighter already."

The children of the family were already much brighter. It was natural enough for them to respond more quickly than their elders to the stimulus of the presence of these kind and helpful strangers, and they were running around, talking to the girls who were preparing dinner, and trying to find some way in which they could help.

And their mother began to forget herself and her troubles, and to watch them with brightening eyes. When she saw that the girls seemed to be fond of her children and to be anxious to make them happy, the maternal instinct in her responded, and was grateful.

"Oh, we're going to be able to bring a lot of cheer and new happiness to these poor people," said Eleanor, confidently. "And it will be splendid, wont it, girls? Could anything be better fun than doing good this way? It's something we'll always be able to remember, and look back at happily. And the strange part of it is that, no matter how much we do for them, we'll be doing more for ourselves."

"Isn't it fine that we've got those blankets?" said Dolly. "If we camp out here to-night they'll be very useful."

"They certainly will. And we shall camp here, though not in tents. Later on this afternoon, we'll have to fix up some sort of shelter. But that will be easy. I'll show you how to do it when the time comes. Now we want to hurry with the dinner—that's the main thing, because I think everyone is hungry."

Jane L. Stewart

CHAPTER IV

GETTING A START

Often people who have been visited by great misfortunes become soured and suspect the motives of even those who are trying to help them. Eleanor understood this trait of human nature very well, thanks to the fact that as a volunteer she had helped out the charity workers in her own city more than once. And as a consequence she did not at all resent the dark looks that were cast at her by the poor woman whose every glance brought home to her more sharply the disaster that the fire had brought.

"We've got to be patient if we want to be really helpful," she explained to Dolly Ransom, who was disposed to resent the woman's unfriendly aspect.

"But I don't see why she has to act as if we were trying to annoy her, Miss Eleanor!"

"She doesn't mean that at all, Dolly. You've never known what it is to face the sort of trouble and anxiety she has had for the last few days. She'll soon change her mind about us when she sees that we are really trying to help. And there's another thing. Don't you think she's a little softer already?"

"Oh, she is!" said Bessie, with shining eyes. "And I think I know why—"

"So will Dolly—if she will look at her now. See, Dolly, she's looking at her children. And when she sees how nice the girls are to them, she is going to be grateful—far more grateful than for anything we did for her. Because, after all, it's probably her fear for her children, and of what this will mean to them, that is her greatest trouble."

Dinner was soon ready, and when it was prepared, Eleanor called the homeless family together and made them sit down.

"We haven't so very much," she said. "We intended to eat just this way, but we were going on a little way. Still, I think there's plenty of everything, and there's lots of milk for the children."

"Why are you so good to us!" asked the woman, suddenly. It was her first admission that she appreciated what was being done, and Eleanor secretly hailed it as a prelude to real friendliness.

"Why, you don't think anyone could see you in so much trouble and not stop to try to help you, do you?" she said.

"Ain't noticed none of the neighbors comin' here to help," said the woman, sullenly.

"I think they're simply forgetful," said Eleanor. "And you know this fire was pretty bad. They had a great fight to save Cranford from burning up."

"Is that so?" said the woman, showing a little interest in the news. "My land, I didn't think the fire would get that far!"

"They were fighting night and day for most of three days," said Eleanor. "And now they're pretty tired, and I have an idea they're making up for lost sleep and rest. But I'm sure you'll find some of them driving out this way pretty soon to see how you are getting on."

"Well, they won't see much!" said the woman, with a despairing laugh. "We came back here, 'cause we thought some of the buildings might be saved. But there ain't a thing left exceptin' that one barn a little way over there. You can't see it from here. It's over the hill. We did save our cattle and a good many chickens and ducks. But all our crops is ruined—and how we are ever goin' to get through the winter I declare I can't tell!"

"Have you a husband? And, by the way, hadn't you better tell me your name!" said Eleanor.

"My husband's dead—been dead nearly two years," said the woman. "I'm Sarah Pratt. This here's my husband's sister, Ann."

"Well, Mrs. Pratt, we'll have to see if we can't think of some way of making up for all this loss," said Eleanor, after she had told the woman her own name, and introduced the girls of the Camp Fire. "Why—just a minute, now! You have cows, haven't you! Plenty of them? Do they give good milk!"

"Best there is," said the woman. "My husband, he was a crank for buyin' fine cattle. I used to tell him he was wastin' his money, but he would do it. Same way with the chickens."

"Then you sold the milk, I suppose?"

"Yes, ma'am, and we didn't get no more for it from the creamery than the farmers who had just the ornery cows."

"Well, I've got an idea already. I'm going back to Cranford as soon as we've had dinner to see if it will work out. I suppose that's your son?"

She looked with a smile at the awkward, embarrassed boy who had so little to say for himself.

"Well, while the girls fix you up some shelters where you can sleep to-night, if you stay here, I'm going to ask you to let him drive me into Cranford. I want to do some telephoning—and I think I'll have good news for you when I come back."

Strangely enough, Mrs. Pratt made no objection to this plan. Once she had begun to yield to the charm of Eleanor's manner, and to believe that the Camp Fire Girls meant really to help and were not merely stopping out of idle curiosity, she recovered her natural manner, which turned out to be sweet and cheerful enough, and she also began to look on things with brighter eyes.

"Makes no difference whether you have good news or not, my dear," she said to Eleanor. "You've done us a sight of good already. Waked me up an' made me see that it's wrong to sit down and cry when it's a time to be up an' doin'."

"Oh, you wouldn't have stayed in the dumps very long," said Eleanor, cheerfully. "Perhaps we got you started a little bit sooner, but I can see that you're not the sort to stay discouraged very long."

Then, while a few of the girls, with the aid of the Pratt children, washed dishes and cleared up after the meal, Eleanor took aside Margery and some of the stronger girls, like Bessie and Dolly, to show them what she wanted done while she was away.

"There's plenty of wood around here," she said. "A whole lot of the boards are only a little bit scorched, and some of them really aren't burned at all. Now, if you take those and lay them against the side of that steep bank there, near where the big barn stood, you'll have one side of a shelter. Then take saplings, and put them up about seven feet away from your boards."

She held a sapling in place, to show what she meant.

"Cut a fork in the top of each sapling, and dig holes so that they will stand up. Then lay strips of wood from the saplings to the tops of your boards, and cover the space you've got that way with branches. If you go about half a mile beyond here, you'll be able to get all the branches you want from spots where the fire hasn't burned at all."

"Why, they'll be like the Indian lean-tos I've read about, won't they?" exclaimed Margery.

"They're on that principle," said Eleanor. "Probably we could get along very well without laying any boards at all against that bank, but it might be damp, and there's no use in taking chances. And—"

"Oh, Miss Eleanor," Dolly interrupted, "excuse me, but if it rained or there were water above, wouldn't it leak right down and run through from the top of the bank?"

"That's a good idea, Dolly. I'll tell you how to avoid that. Dig a trench at the top of the bank, just as long as the shelter you have underneath, and the water will all be caught in that. And if you give the trench a little slope, one way or the other, or both ways from the centre, not much, just an inch in ten feet—the water will all be carried off."

"Oh, yes!" said Dolly. "That would fix that up all right."

"Get plenty of branches of evergreens for the floor, and we'll cover those with our rubber blankets," Eleanor went on. "Then we'll be snug and dry for to-night, anyhow, and for as long as the weather holds fine."

"You mean it will be a place where the Pratts can sleep?" said Margery. "Of course, it would be all right in this weather, but do you think it will stay like this very long?"

"Of course it won't, Margery, but I don't expect them to have to live this way all winter. If it serves to-night and to-morrow night I think it will be all that's needed. Now you understand just what is to be done, don't you? If you want to ask any questions, go ahead."

"No. We understand, don't we, girls?" said Margery.

"All right, then," said Eleanor. "Girls, Margery is Acting Guardian while I'm gone. You're all to do just as she tells you, and obey her just as if she were I. I see that Tom's got the buggy all harnessed up. It's lucky they were able to save their wagons and their horses, isn't it!"

"What are you going to do in Cranford!" asked Dolly. "Won't you tell us, Miss Eleanor?"

"No, I won't, Dolly," said Eleanor, laughing. "If I come back with good news—and I certainly hope I shall—you'll enjoy it all the more if it's a surprise, and if I don't succeed, why, no one will be disappointed except me."

And then with a wave of her hand, she sprang into the waiting buggy and drove off with Tom Pratt holding the reins, and looking very proud of his pretty passenger.

"Well, I don't know what it's all about, but we know just what we're supposed to do, girls," said Margery. "So let's get to work. Bessie, you and Dolly might start picking out the boards that aren't too badly burned."

"All right," said Dolly. "Come on, Bessie!"

"I'll pace off the distance to see how big a place we need to make," said Margery. "Mrs. Pratt, how far is it to a part of the woods that wasn't burned? Miss Mercer thought we could get some green branches there for bedding."

"Not very far," said Mrs. Pratt, with a sigh. "That's what seemed so hard! When we drove along this morning we came quite suddenly to a patch along the road on both sides where the fire hadn't reached, and it made us ever so happy."

"Oh, what a shame!" said Margery. "I suppose you thought you'd come to the end of the burned part?"

"I hoped so—oh, how I did hope so!" said poor Mrs. Pratt. "But then, just before we came in sight of the place, we saw that the fire had changed its direction again, and then we knew that our place must have gone."

"That's very strange, isn't it?" said Margery. "I wonder why the fire should spare some places and not others?"

"It seems as if it were always that way in a big fire," said Mrs. Pratt. "I suppose there'd been some cutting around that patch of woods that wasn't burned. And only last year a man was going to buy the wood in that wood lot of ours on the other side of the road, and clear it. If he had, maybe the fire wouldn't ever have come near us, at all."

"Well, we'll have to think about what did happen, not what

we wish had happened, Mrs. Pratt," said Margery, cheerfully. "The thing to do now is to make the best of a bad business. I'm going to send four or five of the girls to get branches. Perhaps you'll let one of the children go along to show them the way?"

"You go, Sally," said Mrs. Pratt to the oldest girl, a child of fourteen, who had been listening, wide-eyed, to the conversation. "Now, ain't there somethin' Ann an' I can do to help?"

"Why, yes, there is, Mrs. Pratt. I think it's going to be dreadfully hot. Over there, where we unpacked our stores, you'll find a lot of lemons. I think if you'd make a couple of big pails full of lemonade we'd all enjoy them while we were working, and they'd make the work go faster, too."

"The water won't be very cold," suggested Ann.

"Pshaw, Ann! Why not use the ice?" said Mrs. Pratt, whose interest in small things had been wonderfully revived. "The ice-house wasn't burned. Do you go and get a pailful of ice, and we'll have plenty for the girls to drink. They surely will be hot and tired with all they're doing for us."

"I'm sorry I ever said Mrs. Pratt wasn't nice," said Dolly to Bessie, when they happened to overhear this, and saw how Mrs. Pratt began hustling to get the lemonade ready.

"I knew she'd be all right as soon as she began to be waked up a little," said Bessie. "This is more fun than one of our silly adventures, isn't it, Dolly? Because it's just as exciting, but there isn't the chance of things going wrong, and we're doing something to make other people happy."

"You're certainly right about that, Bessie. And it makes you think of how much hard luck people have, and how easy it would be for people who are better off to help them, doesn't it?"

"It *is* easy, Dolly. You know, I think Miss Eleanor must help an awful lot of people. It seems to be the first thing she thinks of when she sees any trouble."

"She makes one understand what Wo-he-lo really means," said Dolly. "She's often explained that work means service— doing things for other people, and not just working for yourself."

"That's one of the things I like best about the Camp Fire," said Bessie, thoughtfully. "Everyone in it seems to be unselfish and to think about helping others, and yet there isn't someone to preach to you all the time—they just do it themselves, and make you see that it's the way to be really happy."

"I wouldn't have believed that I could enjoy this sort of work if anyone had told me so a year ago. But I do. I haven't had such a good time since I can remember. Of course, I feel awfully sorry for the Pratts, but I'm glad that, if it had to happen to them, we came along in time to help them."

They hadn't stopped working while they talked, and now they had brought as many boards as Margery wanted.

"There are lots more boards, Margery," said Dolly. "Why shouldn't we make a sort of floor for the lean-to? If we put up a couple of planks for them to rest on, every so often, we could have a real floor, and then, even if the ground got damp, it would be dry inside."

"Good idea! We'll do that," said Margery, who was busy herself, flying here, there, and everywhere to direct the work.

"Go ahead!"

And so, when the sound of wheels in the road heralded the return of Miss Eleanor in the buggy, the work was done, and the lean-to was completed, a rough-and-ready shelter that was practical in the extreme, though perhaps it was not ornamental.

"Splendid!" cried Eleanor. "But I knew you girls would do well. And I've got the good news I hoped to bring, too!"

CHAPTER V

GOOD NEWS FROM TOWN

Everyone rushed eagerly forward, and crowded around Miss Mercer as she descended from the buggy, smiling pleasantly at the bashful Tom Pratt, who did his best to help her in her descent. And not the least eager, by any means, was Tom Pratt's mother, whose early indifference to the interest of these good Samaritans in her misfortunes seemed utterly to have vanished.

"Oh, these girls of yours!" cried Mrs. Pratt. "You've no idea of how much they've done—or how much they've heartened us all up, Miss Mercer! I don't believe there were ever so many kind, nice people brought together before!"

Eleanor laughed, as if she were keeping a secret to herself. And her words, when she spoke, proved that that was indeed the case.

"Just you wait till you know how many friends you really have around here, Mrs. Pratt!" she said. "Well, I told you I hoped to bring back good news, and I have, and if you'll all give me a chance, I'll tell you what it is."

"You've found a place for all the Pratts to go!" said Dolly.

"You've arranged something so that they won't have to stay here!" agreed Margery.

"I don't know whether Mrs. Pratt would agree that that was such good news," she said. "Tell me, Mrs. Pratt—you are still fond of this place, aren't you?"

"Indeed, and I am, Miss Mercer!" she said, choking back a sob. "When I first saw how it looked this morning, I thought I only wanted to go away and never see it again, if I only knew where to go. But I feel so different now. Why, all the time we've been working around here, it's made me think of how Tom—I mean my poor husband—and I came here when we were first married. Tom had the land, you see, and he'd built a little cabin for us with his own hands."

"And all the farm grew from that?"

"Yes. We worked hard, you see, and the children came, but we had a better place for each one to be born in, Miss Mercer —we really did! It was our place. We've earned it all, with the help from the place itself, and before the fire—"

She broke down then, and for a moment she couldn't go on.

"Of course you love it!" said Eleanor, heartily. "And I don't think it would be very good news for you to know that you had a chance to go somewhere else and make a fresh start, though I could have managed that for you."

"I'd be grateful, though, Miss Mercer," said Mrs. Pratt. "I don't want you to think I wouldn't. It'll be a wrench, though —I'm not saying it wouldn't. When you've lived anywhere as long as I've lived here, and seen all the changes, and had your children born in it, and—"

Jane L. Stewart

"I know—I know," interrupted Eleanor, sympathetically. "And I could see how much you loved the place. So I never had any idea at all of suggesting anything that would take you away."

"Do you really think we can get a new start here?" asked Mrs. Pratt, looking up hopefully.

"I don't only believe it, I know it, Mrs. Pratt," said Eleanor, enthusiastically. "And what's more, you're going to be happier and more prosperous than you ever were before the fire. Not just at first, perhaps, but you're going to see the way clear ahead, and it won't be long before you'll be doing so well that you'll be able to let my friend Tom here go to college."

Mrs. Pratt's face fell. It seemed to her that Eleanor was promising too much.

"I don't see how that could be," she said. "Why, his paw and I used to talk that over. We wanted him to have a fine education, but we didn't see how we could manage it, even when his paw was alive."

"Well, you listen to me, and see if you don't think there's a good chance of it, anyhow," said Eleanor. "In the first place, none of the people in Cranford knew that you'd had all this trouble. It was just as I thought. Their own danger had been so great that they simply hadn't had time to think of anything else. They were shocked and sorry when I told them."

"There's a lot of good, kind people there," said Mrs. Pratt, brightening again. "I'm sure I didn't think anything of their not having come out here to see how we were getting along."

"Some of them would have been out in a day or two, even if

I hadn't told them, Mrs. Pratt. As it is—but I think that part of my story had better wait. Tell me, you've been selling all your milk and cream to the big creamery that supplies the milkmen in the city, haven't you?"

"Yes, and I guess that we can keep their trade, if we can get on our feet pretty soon so that they can get it regular again."

"I've no doubt you could," said Eleanor, dryly. "They make so much money buying from you at cheap prices and selling at high prices that they wouldn't let the chance to keep on slip by in a hurry, I can tell you. But I've got a better idea than that."

Mrs. Pratt looked puzzled, but Tom Pratt, who seemed to be in Eleanor's secret, only smiled and returned Eleanor's wise look.

"When you make butter you salt it and keep it to use here, don't you?" Eleanor asked next.

"Yes, ma'am, we do."

"Well, if you made fresh, sweet butter, and didn't salt it at all, do you know that you could sell it to people in the city for fifty cents a pound?"

Mrs. Pratt gasped.

"Why, no one in the world ever paid that much for butter!" she said, amazed. "And, anyhow, butter without salt's no good."

"Lots of people don't agree with you, and they're willing to pay pretty well to have their own way, too," she said, with a laugh. "In the city rich families think fresh butter is a great luxury, and they can't get enough of it that's really good. And it's the same way, all summer long, at Lake Dean.

"The hotel there will take fifty pounds a week from you all summer long, as long as it's open, that is. And I have got orders for another fifty pounds a week from the people who own camps and cottages. And what's more, the manager of the hotel has another house, in Lakewood, in the winter time, and when he closes up the house at Cranford, he wants you to send him fifty pounds a week for that house, too."

"Why, however did you manage to get all those orders?" asked Margery, amazed.

"I telephoned to the manager of the hotel," said Eleanor. "And then I remembered the girls at Camp Halsted, and I called up Marcia Bates and told her the whole story, and what I wanted them to do. So she and two or three of the others went out in that fast motor boat of theirs and visited a lot of families around the lake, and when they told them about it, it was easy to get the orders."

"Well, I never!" gasped Mrs. Pratt. "I wouldn't ever have thought of doin' anythin' like that, Miss Mercer, and folks around here seem to think I'm a pretty good business woman, too, since my husband died. Why, we can make more out of the butter than we ever did out of a whole season's crops, sellin' at such prices!"

"You won't get fifty cents a pound from the hotel," said Eleanor. "That's because they'll take such a lot, and they'll pay you every week. So I told them they could have all they wanted for forty cents a pound. But, you see, at fifty pounds a week, that's twenty dollars a week, all the year round, and with the other fifty pounds you'll sell to private families, that will make forty-five dollars a week. And you haven't even started yet. You'll have lots more orders than you can fill."

"I'm wonderin' right now, ma'am, how we'll be able to make a hundred pounds of butter a week."

"I thought of that, too," said Eleanor, "and I bought half a dozen more cows for you, right there in Cranford. They're pretty good cows, and if they're well fed, and properly taken care of, they'll be just what you want."

"But I haven't got the money to pay for them now, ma'am!" said Mrs. Pratt, dismayed.

"Oh, I've paid for them," said Eleanor, "and you're going to pay me when you begin to get the profits from this new butter business. I'd be glad to give them to you, but you won't need anyone to give you things; you're going to be able to afford to pay for them yourself."

Mrs. Pratt broke into tears.

"That's the nicest thing you've said or done yet, Miss Mercer," she sobbed. "I just couldn't bear to take charity—"

"Charity? You don't need it, you only need friendly help, Mrs. Pratt, and if I didn't give you that someone else would!"

"And eggs! They'll be able to sell eggs, too, won't they!" said Dolly, jumping up and down in her excitement.

"They certainly will! I was coming to that," said Eleanor. "You know, this new parcel post is just the thing for you, Mrs. Pratt! Just as soon as a letter I wrote is answered, you'll get a couple of cases of new boxes that are meant especially for mailing butter and eggs and things like that from farmers to people in the city.

Jane L. Stewart

"You'll be able to sell eggs and butter cheaper than people in the city can buy things that are anything like as good from the stores, because you won't have to pay rent and lighting bills and all the other expensive things about a city store. I'm going to be your agent, and I do believe I'll make some extra pocket money, too, because I'm going to charge you a commission."

Mrs. Pratt just laughed at that idea.

"Well, you wait and see!" said Eleanor. "I'm glad to be able to help, Mrs. Pratt, but I know you'll feel better if you think I'm getting something out of it, and I'm going to. I think my running across you when you were in trouble is going to be a fine thing for both of us. Why, before you get done with us, you'll have to get more land, and a lot more cows and chickens, because we're going to make it the fashionable thing to buy eggs and butter from you!"

Mrs. Pratt seemed to be overwhelmed, and Eleanor, in order to create a diversion, went over to inspect the lean-to.

"It's just right," she said. "Having a floor made of those boards is a fine idea; I didn't think of that at all. Good for you, Margery!"

"That was Dolly's idea, not mine," said Margery.

"You were perfectly right, too. Well, it's getting a little late and I think it's time we were thinking about dinner. Margery, if you'll go over to the buggy you'll find quite a lot of things I bought in Cranford. We don't want to use up the stores we brought with us before we get away from here. And—here's a secret!"

"What?" said Margery, leaning toward her and smiling. And

Eleanor laughed as she whispered in Margery's ear.

"There are going to be some extra people—at least seven or eight, and perhaps more—for dinner, so we want to have plenty, because I think they're going to be good and hungry when they sit down to eat!"

"Oh, do tell me who they are," cried Margery, eagerly. "I never saw you act so mysteriously before!"

"No, it's a surprise. But you'll enjoy it all the more when it comes for not knowing ahead of time. Don't breathe a word, except to those who help you cook if they ask too many questions."

Dinner was soon under way, and those who were not called upon by Margery busied themselves about the lean-to, arranging blankets and making everything snug for the night.

The busy hands of the Camp Fire Girls had done much to rid the place of its look of desolation, and now everything spoke of hope and renewed activity instead of despair and inaction. A healthier spirit prevailed, and now the Pratts, encouraged as to their future, were able to join heartily in the laughter and singing with which the Camp Fire Girls made the work seem like play.

"Why, what's this?" cried Bessie, suddenly. She had gone toward the road, and now she came running back.

"There are four or five big wagons, loaded with wood and shingles and all sorts of things like that coming in here from the road," she cried. "Whatever are they doing here?"

"That's my second surprise," laughed Eleanor. "It's your neighbors from Cranford, Mrs. Pratt. Don't you recognize

Jud Harkness driving the first team there?"

"Hello, folks!" bellowed Jud, from his seat. "How be you, Mis' Pratt? Think we'd clean forgot you? We didn't know you was in such an all-fired lot of trouble, or we'd ha' been here before. We're come now, though, and we ain't goin' away till you've got a new house. Brought it with us, by heck!"

He laughed as he descended, and stood before them, a huge, black-bearded man, but as gentle as a child. And soon everyone could see what he meant, for the wagons were loaded with timber, and one contained all the tools that would be needed.

"There'll be twenty of us here to-morrow," he said, "and I guess we'll show you how to build a house! Won't be as grand as the hotel at Cranford, mebbe, but you can live in it, and we'll come out when we get the time and put on the finishing touches. To-night we'll clear away all this rubbish, and with sun-up in the morning we'll be at work."

Eleanor's eyes shone as she turned to Mrs. Pratt.

"Now you see what I meant when I told you there were plenty of good friends for you not far from here!" she cried. "As soon as I told Jud what trouble you were in he thought of this, and in half an hour he'd got promises from all the men to put in a day's work fixing up a new house for you."

Mrs. Pratt seemed too dazed to speak.

"But they can't finish a whole house in one day!" declared Margery.

"They can't paint it, and put up wall paper and do everything,

Margery," said Eleanor. "That's true enough. But they can do a whole lot. You're used to thinking of city buildings, and that's different. In the country one or two men usually build a house, and build it well, and when there are twenty or thirty, why, the work just flies, especially when they're doing the work for friendship, instead of because they're hired to do it. Oh, just you wait!"

"Have you ever seen this before!"

"I certainly have! And you're going to see sights to-morrow that will open your eyes, I can promise you. You know what it's like, Bessie, don't you? You've seen house raisings before?"

"I certainly have," said Bessie. "And it's fine. Everyone helps and does the best he can, and it seems no time at all before it's all done."

"Well, we'll do our share," said Eleanor. "The men will be hungry, and I've promised that we'll feed them."

CHAPTER VI

THE GOOD SAMARITANS

"Well, I certainly have got a better opinion of country people than I ever used to have, Bessie," said Dolly Ransom. "After the way those people in Hedgeville treated you and Zara, I'd made up my mind that they were a nasty lot, and I was glad I'd always lived in the city."

"Well, aren't you still glad of it, Dolly? I really do think you're better off in the city. There wouldn't be enough excitement about living in the country for you, I'm afraid."

"Of course there wouldn't! But I think maybe I was sort of unfair to all country people because the crowd at Hedgeville was so mean to you. And I like the country well enough, for a little while. I couldn't bear living there all the time, though. I think that would drive me wild."

"The trouble was that Zara and I didn't exactly belong, Dolly. They thought her father was doing something wrong because he was a foreigner and they couldn't understand his ways."

"I suppose he didn't like them much, either, Bessie."

"He didn't. He thought they were stupid. And, of course, in a way, they were. But not as stupid as he thought they were. He was used to entirely different things, and—oh, well, I suppose in some places what he did wouldn't have been talked about, even.

"But in the country everyone knows the business of everyone else, and when there is a mystery no one is happy until it's solved. That's why Zara and her father got themselves so disliked. There was a mystery about them, and the people in Hedgeville just made up their minds that something was wrong."

"I feel awfully sorry for Zara, Bessie. It must be dreadful for her to know that her father is in prison, and that they are saying that he was making bad money. You don't think he did, do you?"

"I certainly do not! There's something very strange about that whole business, and Miss Eleanor's cousin, the lawyer, Mr. Jamieson, thinks so too. You know that Mr. Holmes is mighty interested in Zara and her father."

"He tried to help to get Zara back to that Farmer Weeks who would have been her guardian if she hadn't come to join the Camp Fire, didn't he?"

"Yes. You see, in the state where Hedgeville is, Farmer Weeks is her legal guardian, and he could make her work for him until she was twenty-one. He's an old miser, and as mean as he can be. But once she is out of that state, he can't touch her, and Mr. Jamieson has had Miss Eleanor appointed her guardian, and mine too, for that state. The state where Miss Eleanor and all of us live, I mean."

"Well, Mr. Holmes is trying to get hold of you, too, isn't he?"

"Yes, he is. You ought to know, Dolly, after the way he tried to get us both to go off with him in his automobile that day, and the way he set those gypsies on to kidnapping us. And that's the strangest thing of all."

"Perhaps he wants to know something about Zara, and thinks you can tell him, or perhaps he's afraid you'll tell someone else something he doesn't want them to know."

"Yes, it may be that. But that lawyer of his, Isaac Brack, who is so mean and crooked that no one in the city will have anything to do with him except the criminals, Mr. Jamieson says, told me once that unless I went with him I'd never find out the truth about my father and mother and what became of them."

"Oh, Bessie, how exciting! You never told me that before. Have you told Mr. Jamieson?"

"Yes, and he just looked at me queerly, and said nothing more about it."

"Bessie, do you know what I think?"

"No. I'm not a mind reader, Dolly!"

"Well, I believe Mr. Jamieson knows more than he has told you yet, or that he guesses something, anyway. And he won't tell you what it is because he's afraid he may be wrong, and doesn't want to raise your hopes unless he's sure that you won't be disappointed."

"I think that would be just like him, Dolly. He's been awfully good to me. I suppose it's because he thinks it will please Miss Eleanor, and he knows that she likes us, and wants to do things for us."

"Oh, I know he likes you, too, Bessie. He certainly ought to, after the way you brought him help back there in Hamilton, when we were there for the trial of those gypsies who kidnapped us. If it hadn't been for you, there's no telling what that thief might have done to him."

"Oh, anyone would have done the same thing, Dolly. It was for my sake that he was in trouble, and when I had a chance to help him, it was certainly the least that I could do. Don't you think so?"

"Well, maybe that's so, but there aren't many girls who would have known how to do what you did or who would have had the pluck to do it, even if they did. I'm quite sure I wouldn't, and yet I'd have wanted to, just as much as anyone."

"I wish I did know something about my father and mother, Dolly. You've no idea how much that worries me. Sometimes I feel as if I never would find out anything."

"Oh, you mustn't get discouraged, Bessie. Try to be as cheerful as you are when it's someone else who is in trouble. You're the best little cheerer-up I know when I feel blue."

"Oh, Dolly, I do try to be cheerful, but it's such a long time since they left me with the Hoovers!"

"Well, there must be some perfectly good reason for it all, Bessie, I feel perfectly sure of that. They would never have gone off that way unless they had to."

"Oh, it isn't that that bothers me. It's feeling that unless something dreadful had happened to them, I'd have heard of them long ago. And then, Maw Hoover and Jake Hoover were always picking at me about them. When I did something Maw Hoover didn't like, she'd say she didn't wonder, that she couldn't expect me to be any good, being the child of parents who'd gone off and left me on her hands that way."

"That's all right for her to talk that way, but she didn't have you on her hands. She made you work like a slave, and never paid you for it at all. You certainly earned whatever they spent for keeping you, Miss Eleanor says so, and I'll take her word any time against Maw Hoover or anyone else."

"I've sometimes thought it was pretty mean for me to run off the way I did, Dolly. If it hadn't been for Zara, I don't believe I'd have done it."

"It's a good thing for Zara that you did. Poor Zara! They'd taken her father to jail, and she was going to have to stay with Farmer Weeks. She'd never have been able to get along without you, you know."

"Well, that's one thing that makes me feel that perhaps it was right for me to go, Dolly. That, and the way Miss Eleanor spoke of it. She seemed to think it was the right thing for me to do, and she knows better than I do, I'm sure."

"Certainly she does. And look here, Bessie! It's all coming out right, sometime, I know. I'm just sure of that! You'll find out all about your father and mother, and you'll see that there was some good reason for their not turning up before."

"Oh, Dolly dear, I'm sure of that now! And it's just that that makes me feel so bad, sometimes. If something dreadful hadn't happened to them, they would have come for me long ago. At least they would have kept on sending the money for my board."

"How do you know they didn't, Bessie? Didn't Maw Hoover get most of the letters on the farm?"

"Yes, she did, Dolly. Paw Hoover couldn't read, so they all went to her, no matter to whom they were addressed."

"Why, then," said Dolly, triumphantly, "maybe your father and mother were writing and sending the money all the time!"

"But wouldn't she have told me so, Dolly?"

"Suppose she just kept the money, and pretended she never got it at all, Bessie? I've heard of people doing even worse things than that when they wanted money. It's possible, isn't it, now? Come on, own up!"

"I suppose it is," said Bessie, doubtfully. "Only it doesn't seem very probable. Maw Hoover was pretty mean to me, but I don't think she'd ever have done anything like that."

"Well, I wouldn't put it above her! She treated you badly enough about other things, heaven knows!"

"I'd hate to think she had done anything quite as mean as that, though, Dolly. I do think she had a pretty hard time herself, and I'm quite sure that if it hadn't been for Jake she wouldn't have been so mean to me."

"Oh, I know just the sort he is. I've seen him, remember, Bessie! He's a regular spoiled mother's boy. I don't know why it is, but the boys whose mothers coddle them and act as if they were the best boys on earth always seem to be the meanest."

"Yes, you did see him, Dolly. Still, Jake's very young, and he wouldn't be so bad, either, if he'd been punished for the things he did at home. As long as I was there, you see, they could blame everything that was done onto me. He did, at least, and Maw believed him."

"Didn't his father ever see what a worthless scamp he was?"

"Oh, how could he, Dolly? He was his own son, you see, and then there was Maw Hoover. She wouldn't let him believe anything against Jake, any more than she would believe it herself."

"I'm sorry for Paw Hoover, Bessie. He seemed like a very nice old man."

"He certainly was. Do you remember how he found me with you girls the day after Zara and I ran away? He could have told them where we were then, but he didn't do it. Instead of that, he was mighty nice to me, and he gave me ten dollars."

"He said you'd earned it, Bessie, and he was certainly right about that. Why, in the city they can't get servants to do all the things you did, even when they're well paid, and you never were paid at all!"

"Well, that doesn't make what he did any the less nice of him, Dolly. And I'll be grateful to him, because he might have made an awful lot of trouble."

"Oh, I'll always like him for that, too. And I guess from what I saw of him, and all I've heard about his wife, that he doesn't have a very happy time at home, either. Maw Hoover must make him do just about what she wants, whether he thinks she's right or not."

"She certainly does, Dolly, unless she's changed an awful lot since I was there."

"Well, I suppose the point is that there really must be more people like him in the country than like his wife and Farmer Weeks. These people around here are certainly being as nice as they can be to the poor Pratts. Just think of their coming here to-morrow to build a new house for them!"

"There are more nice, good-hearted people than bad ones all over, Dolly. That's true of every place, city or country."

"But it seems to me we always hear more of the bad ones, and those who do nasty things, than we do of the others, in the newspapers."

"I think that's because the things that the bad people do are more likely to be exciting and interesting, Dolly. You see, when people do nice things, it's just taken as a matter of course, because that's what they ought to do. And when they do something wicked, it gets everyone excited and makes a lot of talk. That's the reason for that."

"Still, this work that the men from Cranford are going to do for the Pratts is interesting, Bessie. I think a whole lot of people would like to know about that, if there was any way of telling them."

"Yes, that's so. This isn't an ordinary case, by any means. And I guess you'll find that we'll do plenty of talking about it. Miss Eleanor will, I know, because she thinks they ought to get credit for doing it."

"So will Mrs. Pratt and the children, too. Oh, yes, I was wrong about it, Bessie. Lots of people will know about this, because the Pratts will always have the house to remind them of it, and people who go by, if they've heard of it, will remember the story when they see the place. I do wonder what sort of a house they will put up?"

"It'll have to be very plain, of course. And it will look rough at first, because it won't be painted, and there won't be any plaster on the ceilings and there won't be any wall paper, either."

"Oh, but that will be easy to fix later. They'll have a comfortable house for the winter, anyhow, I'm sure. And if they can make as much money out of selling butter and eggs as Miss Eleanor thinks, they'll soon be able to pay to have it fixed up nicely."

"Dolly, I believe we'll be able to help, too. If those girls at Camp Halsted could go around and get so many orders just in an hour or so, why shouldn't we be able to do a lot of it when we get back to the city?"

"Why, that's so, Bessie! I hadn't thought of that. My aunt would buy her butter and eggs there, I know. She's always saying that she can't get really fresh eggs in the city. And they are delicious. That was one of the things I liked best at Miss Eleanor's farm. The eggs there were delicious; not a bit like the musty ones we get at home, no matter how much we pay for them."

"I think it's time we were going to bed ourselves, Dolly. This is going to be like camping out, isn't it?"

"Yes, and we'll be just as comfortable as we would be in tents, too. The Boy Scouts use these lean-tos very often when they are in the woods, you know. They just build them up against the side of a tree."

"I never saw one before, but they certainly are splendid, and they're awfully easy to make."

"We'll have to get up very early in the morning, Bessie. I heard Miss Eleanor say so. So I guess it's a good idea to go to bed, just as you say."

"Yes. The others are all going. We certainly are going to have a busy day to-morrow."

"I don't see that we can do much, Bessie. I know I wouldn't be any good at building a house. I'd be more trouble than help, I'm afraid."

"That's all you know about it! There are ever so many things we can do."

"What, for instance?"

"Well, we'll have to get the meals for the men, and you haven't any idea what a lot of men can eat when they're working hard! They have appetites just like wolves."

"Well, I'll certainly do my best to see that they get enough. They'll have earned it. What else?"

"They'll want people to hand them their tools, and run little errands for them. And if the weather is very hot, they'll be terribly thirsty, too, and we'll be able to keep busy seeing that they have plenty of cooling drinks. Oh, we'll be busy, all right! Come on, let's go to bed."

Jane L. Stewart

CHAPTER VII

THE HOUSE RAISING

The sun was scarcely up in the morning when Eleanor turned out and aroused the girls.

"We've got to get our own breakfast out of the way in a hurry, girls," she said, "When country people say early, they mean early—EARLY! And we want to have coffee and cakes ready for these good friends of ours when they do come. A good many of them will come from a long way off and I think they'll all be glad to have a little something extra before they start work. It won't hurt us a bit to think so, and act accordingly anyhow."

So within half an hour the Pratts and the Camp Fire Girls had had their own breakfasts, the dishes were washed, and great pots of coffee were boiling on the fires that had been built. And, just as the fragrant aroma arose on the cool air, the first of the teams that brought the workers came in sight, with jovial Jud Harkness driving.

"My, but that coffee smells good, Miss Mercer!" he roared. "Say, I'm not strong for all these city fixin's in the way of food. Plain home cookin' serves me well enough, but there's one thing where you sure do lay all over us, and that's in makin' coffee. Give me a mug of that, Mis' Pratt, an' I'll start work."

And from the way in which the coffee and the cakes, the latter spread with good maple syrup from trees that grew near Cranford, began to disappear, it was soon evident that Eleanor had made no mistake, and that the breakfast that she had had prepared for the workers would by no means be wasted.

"It does me good to see you men eat this way," she said, laughing. "That's one thing we don't do properly in the city—eat. We peck at a lot of things, instead of eating a few plain ones, and a lot of them. And I'll bet that you men will work all the harder for this extra breakfast."

"Just you watch and see!" bellowed Jud. "I'm boss here to-day, ma'am, and I tell you I'm some nigger driver. Ain't I, boys?"

But he accompanied the threat with a jovial wink, and it was easy to see that these men liked and respected him, and were only too willing to look up to him as a leader in the work of kindness in which they were about to engage.

"I don't know why all you boys are so good to me, Jud," said Mrs. Pratt, brokenly. "I can't begin to find words to thank you, even."

"Don't try, Mis' Pratt," said Jud, looking remarkably fierce, though he was winking back something that looked suspiciously like a tear. "I guess we ain't none of us forgot Tom Pratt—as good a friend as men ever had! Many's the time he's done kind things for all of us! I guess it'd be pretty poor work if some of his friends couldn't turn out to help his wife and kids when they're in trouble."

"He knows what you're doing, I'm sure of that," she answered. "And God will reward you, Jud Harkness!"

Heartily as the men ate, however, they spent little enough time at the task. Jud Harkness allowed them what he thought was a reasonable time, and then he arose, stretched his great arms, and roared out his commands.

"Come on, now, all hands to work!" he bellowed. "We've got to get all this rubbish cleared out, then we'll have clean decks for building."

And they fell to with a will. In a surprisingly short space of time the men who had plunged into the ruined foundations of the house had torn out the remaining beams and rafters, and had flung the heap of rubbish that filled the cellar on to the level ground. While some of the men did this, others piled the rubbish on to wagons, and it was carted away and dumped. The fire, however, had really lightened their task for them.

"That fire was so hot and so fierce," said Eleanor, as she watched them working, "that there's less rubbish, than if the things had been only half burned."

"I've seen fires in the city," said Margery, "or, at least, houses after a fire. And it really looked worse than this, because there'd be a whole lot of things that had started to burn. Then the firemen came along, to put out the fire, and, though the things weren't really any good, they had to be carted away."

"Yes, but this fire made a clean sweep wherever it started at all. Ashes are easier to handle than sticks and half ruined pieces of furniture. As long as it had to come, I guess it's a good thing that it was such a hot blaze."

The work of clearing away, therefore, which had to be done, of course, before any actual building could be begun, was soon accomplished.

"We're going to build just the way Tom Pratt did," said Jud Harkness. He was the principal carpenter and builder of Lake Dean, and a master workman. Many of the camps and cottages on the lake had been built by him, and he was, therefore, accustomed to such work.

"You mean you're going to put up a square house?" said Eleanor.

"Yes, ma'am, just a square house, with a hall running right through from the front to the back, and an extension in the rear for a kitchen—just a shack, that will be. Two floors—two rooms on each side of the hall on each floor. That'll give them eight rooms to start with, beside the kitchen."

"That'll be fine, and it will really be the easiest thing to do, too."

"That's what we're figuring, ma'am. You see, it'll be just as it was when Tom Pratt first built here, except that he only put up one story at first. Then, as Mis' Pratt gets things going again, she can add to it, and if she don't get along as fast as she expects, why, we'll lend her a hand whenever she needs it."

"How on earth could you get all the lumber you need ready so quickly? That's one thing I couldn't understand. The work is not so difficult to manage, of course. But the wood—that's what's been puzzling me."

Jud grinned.

"Well, the truth is, ma'am, I expect to have a little argument about that yet with a city chap that's building a house on the lake. I've got the job of putting it up for him, and if it hadn't been for this fire coming along, I'd have started work day before yesterday."

"Oh, and this is the lumber for his house?"

"You guessed it right, ma'am! He'll be wild, I do believe, because there's no telling when I'll get the next lot of lumber through."

"You say the fire stopped you from going ahead with his house?"

"Yes. You see all of us had to turn out when it got so near to Cranford. My house is safe, I do believe. I'm mighty scared of fire, ma'am, and I've always figured on having things fixed so's a fire would have a pretty hard time reaching my property. But of course I had to jump in to help my neighbors—wouldn't be much profit about having the only house left standing in town, would there?"

Eleanor laughed.

"I guess not!" she said. "But what a lucky thing for Mrs. Pratt that you happened to have just the sort of wood she needed!"

"Oh, well, we'd have managed somehow. Of course, it makes it easier, but we'd have juggled things around some way, even if this chap's plans didn't fit her foundations. As it happens, though, they do. Old Tom Pratt had a mighty well-built house here."

"Well, I'm quite sure that just as good a one is going up in its place."

Jud Harkness watched the work of getting out the last of the rubbish. Then he went over to the cleared foundations, and in a moment he was putting up the first of the four corner posts, great beams that looked stout enough to hold up a far bigger house than the one they were to support.

All morning the work went on merrily. As Eleanor had predicted, and Bessie, too, there was plenty for the girls to do. The sun grew hotter and hotter, and the men were glad of the cooling drinks that were so liberally provided for them.

"This is fine!" said Jud Harkness, as he quaffed a great drink of lemonade, well iced. "My, but it's a pleasure to work when it's made so nice for you! I tell you, having these cool drinks here is worth an extra hour's work, morning and afternoon. And what's that—just the nails I want? I'll give you a job as helper, young woman!"

That remark was addressed to Bessie, who flushed with pleasure at the thought that she was playing a part, however small, in the building of the house. And, indeed, the girls all did their part, and their help was royally welcomed by the men.

Quickly the skeleton of the house took form, and by noon, when work was to be knocked off for an hour, the whole framework was up.

"I simply wouldn't have believed it, if I hadn't seen it with my own eyes!" said Eleanor. "It's the most wonderful thing I ever saw!"

"Oh, shucks!" said Jud, embarrassed by such, praise. "There's lots of us—I don't think we've done so awful well.

But it does look kind of nice, don't it?"

"It's going to be a beautiful house," said Mrs. Pratt. "And to think of what the place looked like yesterday! Well, Jud Harkness, I haven't any words to tell you what I really think, and that's all there is to it!"

For an hour or more Margery and her helpers had been busy at the big fire. At Eleanor's suggestion two of the men had stopped work on the house long enough to put up a rough, long table with benches at the sides, and now the table was groaning with the fine dinner that Margery had prepared.

"Good solid food—no fancy fixings!" Eleanor had decreed. "These men burn up a tremendous lot of energy in work, and we've got to give them good food to replace it. So we don't want a lot of trumpery things, such as we like!"

She had enforced a literal obedience, too. There were great joints of corned beef, red and savory; pots of cabbage, and huge mounds of boiled potatoes. Pots of mustard were scattered along the table, and each man had a pitcher of fine, fresh milk, and a loaf of bread, with plenty of butter. And for dessert there was a luxury—the only fancy part of the meal.

Eleanor had had a whispered conference with Tom Pratt early in the day, as the result of which he had hitched up and driven into Cranford, to return with two huge tubs of ice-cream. He had brought a couple of boxes of cigars, too, and when the meal was over, and the men were getting out their pipes, Eleanor had gone around among them.

"Try one of these!" she had urged. "I know they're good—and I know that when men are working hard they enjoy a first-class smoke."

The cigars made a great hit.

"By Golly! There's nothing she don't think of, that Miss Mercer!" said Jud Harkness appreciatively, as he lit up, and sent great clouds of blue smoke in the air. "Boys, if we don't do a tiptop job on that house to finish it off this afternoon we ought to be hung for a lot of ungrateful skunks. Eh?"

There was a deep-throated shout of approval for that sentiment, and, after a few minutes of rest, during which the cigars were enjoyed to the utmost, Jud rose and once more sounded the call to work.

"I've heard men in the city say that after a heavy meal in the middle of the day, they couldn't work properly in the afternoon," said Eleanor, as she watched the men go about their work, each seeming to know his part exactly. "It doesn't seem to be so with these men, though, does it? I guess that in the city men who work in offices don't use their bodies enough—they don't get enough exercise, and they eat as much as if they did."

"I love cooking for men who enjoy their food the way these do," said Margery happily. "They don't have to say it's good —they show they think so by the way they eat. It's fine to think that people really enjoy what you do. I don't care how hard I work if I think that."

"Well, you certainly had an appreciative lot of eaters to-day, Margery."

As the shadows lengthened and the sun began to go down toward the west the house rapidly assumed the look it would have when it was finished. A good deal of the work, of course, was roughly done. There was no smoothing off of rough edges, but all that could be done later.

Jane L. Stewart

And then, as the end of the task drew near, so that the watchers on the ground could see what the finished house would be like, Mrs. Pratt, already overwhelmed by delight at the kindness of her neighbors, had a new surprise that pleased and touched her, if possible, even more than what had gone before. A new procession of wagons came into sight in the road, and this time each was driven by a woman.

And what a motley collection of stuff they did bring, to be sure! Beds and mattresses, bedding, chairs, tables, a big cook stove for the kitchen, pots and pans, china and glass, knives and forks—everything that was needed for the house.

"We just made a collection of all the things we could spare, Sarah Pratt," said sprightly little Mrs. Harkness, a contrast indeed to her huge husband, who could easily lift her with one hand, so small was she. "They ain't much on looks, but they're all whole and clean, and you can use them until you have a chance to stock up again. Now, don't you go trying to thank us—it's nothing to do!"

"Nothing?" exclaimed Mrs. Pratt. "Sue Harkness, don't you dare say that! Why, it means that I'll have a real home to-night for my children—we'll be jest as comfortable as we were before the fire! I don't believe any woman ever had such good neighbors before!"

Long before dark the house was finished, as far as it was to be finished that day. And, as soon as the men had done their work, their wives and the Camp Fire Girls descended on the new house with brooms and pails, and soon all the shavings and the traces of the work had been banished. Then all hands set to work arranging the furniture, and by the time supper was ready the house was completely furnished.

"Well," said Eleanor, standing happily in the parlor, "this

certainly does look homelike!"

There was even an old parlor organ. Pictures were on the wall; a good rag carpet was on the floor, and, while the furniture was not new, and had seen plenty of hard service, it was still good enough to use. The Pratt home had certainly risen like a Phoenix from its ashes. And tired but happy, all those who had contributed to the good work sat down to a bountiful supper.

Jane L. Stewart

CHAPTER VIII

ON THE MARCH AGAIN

After supper, when the others who had done the good work of rebuilding were ready to go, all the girls of the Camp Fire lined up in front of the new house and sped them on their way with a cheer and the singing of the Wo-he-lo cry.

"Listen to that echo!" said Dolly, as their song was brought back to them. "I didn't notice that last night. Is it always that way?"

"Always," said Tom Pratt. "Folks come here sometimes to yell and hear the echo shout back at them."

"Good!" cried Eleanor. "That supplies a need I've been thinking of all day!"

"What's that, Miss Mercer?" asked Mrs. Pratt.

"Why, if you are going into the business of supplying eggs and butter to the summer folk at the lake and to others in the city, you'll need a name for your farm. Why not call it Echo Farm? That's a good name, and in your case it means something, you see."

"Whatever you say, Miss Mercer! Though I'd never thought of having a name for the place before."

"Lots of things are going to be different for you now, Mrs. Pratt. You're going to be a business woman, and to make a lot of money, you know. Yes, that will look well on your boxes. When I get back to the city I'll have a friend of mine make a drawing and put that name with it, to be put on your boxes, and on all the paper you will use for writing letters."

"Dear me, it's going to be splendid, Miss Mercer! Why, that fire is going to turn out to be the best thing that ever happened to us, I'm sure!"

"I think we can often turn our misfortunes into blessings if we take them the right way, Mrs. Pratt. The thing to do is always to try to look on the bright side, and, no matter how black things seem, to try to see if there isn't some way that we can turn everything to account."

"Well, I would never have done it if you hadn't come along, Miss Mercer. You gave us all courage in the first place, and then you got Jud Harkness and all the others to come and help me this way."

"Oh, they'd have done it themselves, as soon as they heard. I didn't suggest a thing—I just told them the news, and they thought of everything else all by themselves. The only thing I thought of was using your farm so that it would really pay you."

"Now that you've told us how, it seems so easy that I wonder I never thought of it myself."

"Well, lots and lots of farmers just waste their land and themselves, Mrs. Pratt. You're not the only one. My father

Jane L. Stewart

has a farm, and in his section he's done his level best to make the regular farmers see that there are new ways of farming, just as there are new ways of doing everything else."

"That's what my poor husband always said. He had all sorts of new-fangled ideas, as I used to call them. Maybe he was right, too. But he didn't have money enough to try them and see how they'd do, though we always made a good living off this place."

"Well, the advantage of my idea is that you don't need much money to give it a trial, and if you don't succeed, you won't lose much."

"I think we'd be pretty stupid if we didn't succeed, after the fine start you've given us, and the way you've told me what to do."

"Well, I think so myself," said Eleanor, with a frank laugh. "And I know you're not stupid—not a bit of it! It's going to be hard work, but I'm sure you'll succeed. You'll be able to hire someone to do most of the work for you before long, I think, and then you'll have to have a rest, and come down to visit me in the city."

"Well, well, I do hope so, Miss Mercer! I ain't been in the city since I don't know when. Tom—my husband—took me once, but that was years and years ago, and I expect there's been a lot of changes since then."

"I'm going to keep an eye on you, Mrs. Pratt. And I feel as if I were a sort of partner in this business, so if you don't make as much money as I think you ought to, why, you'll hear from me. I can promise you that! Girls, we'll sleep in the lean-to to-night, and in the morning we'll be off, bright and early."

"Oh," said Mrs. Pratt, "have you really got to go? And you'll not sleep out to-night! You'll take the house, and we'll be the ones to sleep outside."

"Nonsense, Mrs. Pratt! Who should be the ones to sleep in this fine new house the first night but you? We love to sleep in the open air, really we do! It's no hardship, I can tell you."

And, despite all of Mrs. Pratt's protests, it was so arranged.

"I'll hate to go away from here—really I will!" said Dolly, to Bessie. "It's been perfectly fine, helping these people. And I feel as if we'd really done something."

"Well, we certainly have, Dolly," said Bessie.

"I do hope that butter and egg business will do well."

"I *know* it's going to do well," said Eleanor, who had over-heard. "And one reason is that you girls are going to help. Now we must all get to sleep, or we'll never get started in the morning. I think we'll have to ride part of the way to the seashore in the train, after all. We don't want to be too late in getting there, you know."

And in a few minutes silence reigned over the place. It was a picture of peace and content—a vast contrast to the scene of the previous night, when desolation and gloom seemed to dominate everything.

Parting in the morning brought tears alike to the eyes of those who stayed behind and those who were going on. The experience of the last two days had brought the Pratts and the girls of the Camp Fire very close together, and the Pratt children—the younger ones at least—wept and refused to be comforted when they learned that their new friends were going away.

"Cheer up," said Eleanor. "We'll see you again, you know. Maybe we'll all come up next summer. And we've had a good time, haven't we?"

"We certainly have!" said Mrs. Pratt, and there was sincerity, as well as pleasure, in her tone. "I've often heard that good came out of evil, and joy out of sorrow, but I never had any such reason to believe it before this!"

Before the final parting, Eleanor had shown Mrs. Pratt exactly what she meant about the new way in which the butter was to be made.

"Of course, as your business grows, you will want to get better machinery," she had said. "That will make the work much easier, and you will be able to do it more quickly too, and with less help than if you stuck to the old-fashioned way."

"I'm going to take your advice in everything about running this farm, Miss Mercer," Mrs. Pratt had replied. "You've certainly shown that you know what you're talking about so far."

"Take a trip down to my father's farm some time, Mrs. Pratt, and they'll be glad to show you everything they have there, I know. My father is very anxious for all the farmers in his neighborhood to profit by any help they can get. The only trouble is that a good many of them seem to feel that he is interfering with them."

"Well, if they're as stupid as that, it serves them right to keep on losing money, Miss Mercer."

"But it's natural, after all. You see they've run their farms their own way all their lives, and it's the way they learned from their fathers. So it isn't very strange that they're apt to feel that they know more, from all that practice and experiment, than city people who are farming scientifically."

"Does your father enjoy farming?"

"He says he does—and it's a curious thing that he makes that farm pay its way, even allowing for a whole lot of things he does that aren't really necessary. That's what proves, you see, that his theories are right—they pay.

"Of course, he could afford to lose money on it, and you can't make a whole lot of those farmers in our neighborhood believe that he doesn't. So now he is having the books of the farm fixed up so that any of the farmers around can see them, and find out for themselves how things are run."

Tired as the girls of the Camp Fire had been the night before, they were wonderfully refreshed by their night's sleep. The weather was much more pleasant than it had been, and a brisk wind had driven off much of the smoke that still remained when they reached the Pratt farm as a reminder of the scourge of fire. So the conditions for walking were good, and Eleanor Mercer set a round, swinging pace as they started off.

"I'll really be glad to get out of this burned district. It's awfully gloomy, isn't it, Bessie?" said Dolly.

"Yes, especially when you realize what it means to the people who live in the path of the fire," answered Bessie. "Seeing the Pratts as they were when we came up has given me an altogether new idea of these forest fires."

"Yes. That's what I mean. It's bad enough to see the forest ruined, but when you think of the houses, and all the other things that are burned, too, why, it seems particularly dreadful."

"Tom Pratt told me that a whole lot of animals were caught in the fire, too—chipmunks, and squirrels, and deer. That seems dreadful."

"Oh, what a shame! I should think they could manage to get away, Bessie. Don't you suppose they try?"

"Oh, yes, but you see they can't reason the way human beings do, and a lot of these fires burn around in a circle, so that while they were running away from one part of the fire they might very easily be heading straight for another, and get caught right between two fires."

Soon, however, they passed a section where the land had been cleared of trees for a space of nearly a mile, and, once they had travelled through it, they came to the deep green woods again, where no marring traces of the fire spoiled the beauty of their trip.

"Ah, don't the woods smell good!" said Dolly. "So much nicer than that old smoky smell! I never smelt anything like that! It got so that everything I ate tasted of smoke. I'm certainly glad to get to where the fire didn't come."

Now the ground began to rise, and before long they found themselves in the beginning of Indian Gap. The ground rose gradually, and when they stopped for their midday meal, in a wild part of the gap, none of the girls were feeling more than normally and healthfully tired.

"Do many people come through here, Miss Eleanor?"

asked Margery.

"At certain times, yes. But, you see, the forest fires have probably made a lot of people who intended to take this trip change their minds. In a way it's a good thing, because we will be sure to find plenty of room at the Gap House. That's where we are to spend the night. Sometimes when there's a lot of travel, it's very crowded there, and uncomfortable."

"Is it a regular hotel?"

"No, it's just a place for people to sleep. It's where the trail starts up Mount Sherman, and it's the station of the railroad that runs to the top of the mountain, too, for people who are too lazy to climb. There's a gorgeous view there in the mornings, when the sun rises. You can see clear to the sea."

"Oh, can't we stop and see that?"

"We haven't time to climb the mountain. If you want to go up on the incline railway, though, we can manage it. You get up at three o'clock in the morning, and get to the top while it's still dark, so that you can see the very beginning of the sunrise."

There was not a dissenting voice to the plan to make the trip, and it was decided to take the little extra time that would be required.

"After all," said Eleanor, "we can get such an early start afterward that it won't take very much time. And to-morrow we'll finish our tramp through the gap, and stop at Windsor for the night. Then the next day we'll take the train straight through to the seashore. I think really we'll have more fun, and get more good out of it if we spend the time there than if we go through with our original plan of doing more walking before getting on the train."

"Yes. We've lost quite a little time already, haven't we?" said Margery.

"Two whole days at Lake Dean, and two days more staying with the Pratts," said Eleanor. "That's four days, and one can walk quite a long distance in four days if one sets one's mind and one's feet to it."

"Well, we certainly couldn't help the delay," said Margery. "At Lake Dean the fire held us—and I wouldn't think very much of any crowd that could see the trouble those poor people were in and not stay to help them."

They slept well in the early part of that night in the rough quarters at the Gap House, and, while it was still dark, they were routed out to catch the funicular railway on its first trip of the day up Mount Sherman.

At first, when they were at the top of the mountain, there was nothing to be seen. But soon the sky in the east began to lighten and grow pink, then the fog that lay below them began to melt away, and, as the sun rose, they saw the full wonder of the spectacle.

"I never saw anything so beautiful in all my life!" exclaimed Bessie with a sigh of delight. "See how it seems to gild everything as the light rises, Dolly!"

"Yes, and you can see the sea, way off in the distance! How tiny all the towns and villages look from here! It's just like looking at a map, isn't it?"

"Well, it was certainly worth getting up in the middle of the night to see it, Bessie. And I do love to sleep, too!"

"I'd stay up all night to see this, any time. I never even dreamed of anything so lovely."

"We were very fortunate," said Eleanor, with a smile. "I've been up here when the fog was so thick that you couldn't see a thing, and only knew the sun had risen because it got a little lighter. I've known it to be that way for a week at a time, and some people would stay, and come up here morning after morning, and be disappointed each time!"

"That's awfully mean," said Dolly. "I suppose, though, if they had never seen it, they wouldn't mind so much, because they wouldn't know what they were missing."

"They never seemed very happy about it, though," laughed Eleanor. "Well, it's time to go down again, and be off for Windsor. And then to-morrow morning we'll be off for the seashore. We're to camp there, right on the beach, instead of living in a house. That will be much better, I think."

CHAPTER IX

A STARTLING DISCOVERY

"Bessie, why are you looking so glum?" asked Dolly, as they started on the last part of their walk, taking the Windsor road.

"Am I? I didn't realize I was, Dolly. But—well, I suppose it's because I'm rather sorry we're leaving the mountains."

"I think the seashore is every bit as nice as the mountains. There are ever so many things to do, and I know you'll like Plum Beach, where we're going. It's the dandiest place—"

"It couldn't be as nice as this, Dolly."

"Oh, that seems funny to me, Bessie. I've always loved the seashore, ever since I can remember. And, of course, since I've learned to swim, I've enjoyed it even more than I used to."

"You can't swim much in the sea, can you? Isn't the surf too heavy?"

"The surf's good fun, even if you don't do any swimming in it, Bessie. It picks you up and throws you around, and it's splendid sport. But down at Plum Beach you can have either still water or surf. You see, there's a beach and a big cove— and on that beach the water is perfectly calm, unless there's a tremendous storm, and we're not likely to run into one of those."

"How is that, Dolly? I thought there was always surf at the seashore."

"There's a sand bar outside the cove, and it's grown so that it really makes another beach, outside. And on that there is real surf. So we can have whichever sort of bathing we like best, or both kinds on the same day, if we want."

"Maybe I'll like it better when I see it, then. Because I do love to swim, and I don't believe I'd enjoy just letting the surf bang me around."

"Why, Bessie, you say you may like it better when you see it? Haven't you ever been to the seashore?"

"I certainly never have, Dolly! You seem to forget that I've spent all the time I can remember in Hedgeville."

"I do forget it, all the time. And do you know why? It's because you seem to know such an awful lot about other places and things you never saw there. I suppose they made you read books."

"Made me! That was one of the things Maw Hoover used to get mad at me for doing. Whenever she saw me reading a book it seemed to make her mad, and she'd say I was loafing, and find something for me to do, even if I'd hurried through all the chores I had so that I could get at the book sooner."

"Then you used to like to read?"

Jane L. Stewart

"Oh, yes, I always did. The Sunday School had a sort of library, and I used to be able to get books from there. I love to read, and you would, too, Dolly, if you only knew how much fun you have out of books."

Dolly made a face.

"Not the sort of books my Aunt Mabel wants me to read," she said decidedly. "Stupid old things they are! It's just like going to school all over again. I get enough studying at school, thanks!"

"But you like to know about people and places you've never seen, don't you!"

"Yes, but all the books I've ever seen that tell you about things like that are just like geographies. They give you a lot of things you have to remember, and there's no fun to that."

"You haven't read the right sort of books, that's all that's the matter with you, Dolly. I tell you what—when we get back to the city, we '11 get hold of some good books, and take turns reading them aloud to one another. I think that would be good fun."

"Well, maybe if they taught me as much as you seem to know about places you've never seen I wouldn't mind reading them. Anyhow, books or no books, you're going' to love the seashore. Oh, it is such a delightful place—Plum Beach."

"Tell me about it, Dolly."

"Well, in the first place, it isn't a regular seaside place at all. I mean there aren't any hotels and boardwalks and things like that. It's about ten miles from Bay City, and there they do have everything like that. But Plum Beach is just wild, the way it always has been. And I don't see why, because it's the best beach I ever saw—ever so much finer than at Bay City."

"I'll like the beach."

"Yes, I know you will. And because it's sort of wild and desolate, and off by itself that way, you can have the best time there you ever dreamed of. Last year we put on our bathing suits when we got up, and kept them on all day. You go in the water, you see, and then, if you lie down on the beach for half an hour, you're dry. The sun shines right down on the sand, and it's as warm as it can be."

"I suppose that's why you like it so much—because you don't have the trouble of dressing and undressing."

"It's one reason," said Dolly, who never pretended about anything, and was perfectly willing to admit that she was lazy. "But it's nice to have the beach to yourselves, too, the way we do. You see, when we get there we'll find tents all set up and ready for us."

"Is there any fishing?"

Dolly smacked her lips.

"You bet there is!" she said. "Best sea bass you ever tasted, and about all you can catch, too! And it tastes delicious, because the fish down there get cooked almost as soon as they're caught. And there are lobsters and crabs—and it's good fun to go crabbing. Then at low tide we dig for clams, and they're good, too—I'll bet you never dreamed how good a clam could be!"

"How about the other things—milk, and eggs, and all those!"

"Oh, that's easy! There are a lot of farms a little way inland, and we get all sorts of fine things from them."

"I wonder if Mr. Holmes will try to play any tricks on us down there, Dolly. He has about everywhere we've been since Zara and I joined the Camp Fire Girls, you know."

"I'm hoping he won't find out, Bessie. That would be fine. I certainly would like to know why he is so anxious to get hold of you and Zara. I bet it's money, and that there's some secret about you."

"Money? Why, he's got more than he can spend now! Even if there is a secret, I don't see how money can have anything to do with it."

"Well, you remember this, Bessie: the more money people have, the more they seem to want. They're never content. It's the people who only have a little who seem to be happy, and willing to get along with what they have. How about your old Farmer Weeks?"

"That's so, Dolly. He certainly was that way. He had more money than anyone in Hedgeville or anywhere near it, and yet he was the stingiest, closest fisted old man in town."

"There you are!"

"Still I think Mr. Holmes must be a whole lot richer than Farmer Weeks, or than all the other people in Hedgeville put together. And it doesn't seem as if there was any money he could make out of Zara or me that would tempt him to do what he's done."

"Do you know what I've noticed most, Bessie, about the way he's gone to work?"

"No. What?"

"The way he has spent money. He's acted as if he didn't care a bit how much it cost him, if only he got what he wanted. And people in the city never spend money unless they expect to get it back."

"Who's the detective now! You called me one a little while ago, but it seems to me that you're doing pretty well in that line yourself."

"Oh, it's all right to laugh, but, just the same, I'll bet that when we get at the bottom of all this mystery, we'll find that the chief reason Mr. Holmes was in it was that he wanted to get hold of some information that would make it easy for him to get a whole lot more than it cost him."

"Well, maybe you're right, Dolly. But I'd certainly like to know just what he has got up his sleeve."

"I think he'll be careful for a little while now, Bessie. He never knew that Miss Eleanor had that letter he'd written to the gypsy. And it must have damaged him a lot to have as much come out about that as did."

"I expect a lot of people who heard it didn't believe it."

"Even if that's so, I guess there were plenty who did believe it, and who think now that Mr. Holmes is a pretty good man to leave alone. You see, that proved absolutely that he had really hired that gypsy to carry you off, and that is a pretty mean thing to do. And people must know by this time that if there was any legal way of getting you and Zara away from the Camp Fire and Miss Mercer, he would do it."

"But he didn't get into any trouble for doing it, Dolly."

Jane L. Stewart

"He's got so much money that he could hire lawyers to get him out of almost any scrape he got in, Bessie. That's the trouble. Those people at Hamilton were afraid of him. They know how rich he is, and they didn't want to take any chance of making him angry at them."

"Yes, that's just it. And I'm afraid he's got so much money that a whole lot of people who would say what they really thought if they weren't afraid of him, are on his side. You see, he says that I'm a runaway, just because I didn't stay any longer with the Hoovers. And probably he can make a whole lot of people think that I was very ungrateful, and that he is quite right in trying to get me back into the same state as Hedgeville."

"They'd better talk to Miss Eleanor, if he makes them think that. They'll soon find out which is right and which is wrong in that business. And if she doesn't tell them, I guess Mr. Jamieson will—and he'd be glad of the chance, too!"

"Let's not worry about him, anyhow. I hope he won't find out where we are, too. We haven't seen or heard anything of him since we went back to Long Lake from Hamilton, so I don't see why there isn't a good chance of his letting us alone for a while now."

They reached Windsor, the little town at the other end of Indian Gap, late in the afternoon, having cooked their midday meal in the gap.

"I know the people in a big boarding-house here," said Eleanor, "and we'll be very comfortable. In the morning we'll take an early train, so that we can get to Plum Beach before it's too late to get comfortably settled. I've sent word on ahead to have the tents ready for us, but, even so, there will be a good many things to do."

"There always are," sighed Dolly. "That's the one thing I don't like about camping out."

"I expect really, if you only knew the truth, Dolly, it's the one thing you like best of all," smiled Eleanor. "That's one of the great differences between being at home, where everything is done for you, and camping out, where you have to look after yourself."

"Well, I don't like work, anyhow, and I don't believe I ever shall, Miss Eleanor, no matter what it's called. Some of it isn't as bad as some other kinds, that's all."

Eleanor laughed to herself, because she knew Dolly well enough not to take such declarations too seriously.

"I've got some work for you to-night," she said. "I want you and Bessie to go to a meeting of the girls that belong to one of the churches here, and tell them about the Camp Fire. They found out we were coming, and they would like to know if they can't start a Camp Fire of their own.

"And I think they'll get a better idea of things, and be less timid and shy about asking questions if two of you girls go than if I try to explain. I will come in later, after they've had a chance to talk to you two, but by that time they ought to have a pretty clear idea."

"That's not work, that's fun," declared Dolly.

"I'm glad you think so, because you will be more likely to be successful."

And so after supper Bessie and Dolly went, with two girls who called for them, to the Sunday School room of one of the Windsor churches, ready to do all they could to induce the local girls to form a Camp Fire of their own. And, being thoroughly enthusiastic, they soon fired the desire of the Windsor girls.

"They won't have just one Camp Fire; they'll have two or three," predicted Dolly, when she and Bessie were walking back to the boarding-house later with Eleanor Mercer. "They asked plenty of questions, all right. Nothing shy about them, was there, Bessie?"

Bessie laughed.

"Not if asking questions proves people aren't shy," she admitted. "I thought they'd never stop thinking of things to ask."

"That's splendid," said Eleanor. "The Camp Fire is the best thing these girls could have. It will do them a great deal of good, and I was sure that the way to make them see how much they would enjoy it was to let them understand how enthusiastic you two were. That meant more to them than anything I could have said, I'm sure."

"I don't see why," said Dolly.

"Because they're girls like you, Dolly, and it's what you like, and show you like, that would appeal to them. I'm older, you see, and they might think that things that I would expect them to like wouldn't really please them at all."

"What's the matter with you, Bessie?" asked Dolly suddenly, as they reached the house. She was plainly concerned and surprised, and Eleanor, rather startled, since she had seen nothing in Bessie to provoke such a question, looked at her keenly.

"Nothing, except that I'm a little tired, I think."

But Dolly wasn't satisfied. She knew her chum too well.

"You've got something on your mind, but you don't want to worry us," she said. "Better own up, Bessie!"

Bessie, however, would not answer. And in the morning she seemed to be her old self. Just as they were starting for the train, though, Bessie suddenly hung back at the door of the boarding-house.

"Wait for me a minute, Dolly," she said. "I left a handkerchief in our room. I'll be right down. Go on, the rest of you; we'll soon catch up."

She ran upstairs for the handkerchief.

"I left it behind on purpose, Dolly," she explained, when she came down. "I wanted them to go ahead. Ah, look!"

As they went along, with most of the girls fully a hundred yards ahead of them, a lurking figure was plainly to be seen following the girls.

"It's Jake Hoover!" said Dolly excitedly.

"I thought I saw him last night. That was why you thought something was wrong, Dolly," said Bessie. "But I wanted to make sure before I said anything."

"That means trouble," said Dolly.

CHAPTER X

A MEETING—AND A CONVERSION

"Trouble—he's always meant that every time we've seen him!" said Bessie bitterly.

"How do you suppose he has managed to be away from home so much, Bessie?"

"I don't know, Dolly, but I'm afraid he's got into some sort of trouble. I'm quite sure that Mr. Holmes and that lawyer, Mr. Brack, have got something against him—that they know something he's afraid they will tell."

"Say, I'll bet you're right! You know, he must be an awful coward—and yet, the way he goes after you, he takes a lot of chances, doesn't he? It does look as if, no matter how much it may frighten him to do what he does, he's still more afraid not to do it."

"Look out—get behind this tree! I don't want him to see us here if we can help it. It would be better if he thought he hadn't been noticed at all, don't you think?"

"Yes. And it's a very good thing we saw him, Bessie. Now we know that we must look out for squalls at Plum Beach, and they don't know we're warned at all. So maybe it will be easier to beat them."

"Look here, Dolly, isn't there another train to Plum Beach? A later one, that would get us there an hour or so after the other girls, if they go on this one?"

"There certainly is, Bessie; but how can we wait for it? Miss Eleanor would be worried."

"Oh, we'll have to let her know what we're going to do, of course. How soon does that train go?"

"Not for half an hour yet. Miss Mercer wanted to be at the station very early so that all the baggage would surely be checked in time to go on the same train with us."

"Well, that makes it easy, Dolly. I tell you what. I'll stay here, and follow very slowly, when Jake gets out of sight, so that he won't see me. And if you go right across the street, and cut across the lots there, you can get to the railroad station from the other side."

"I know the way—I saw that last night, though not because I expected to do it."

"All right, then. You take that way, and get hold of Miss Eleanor quietly. Better not let the others hear what you're saying, and keep your eyes open for Jake, too. But I don't believe he'll show himself in the station."

"Do you think she'll let us do it!"

"I don't see why not. We'll be perfectly safe. I'm sure Jake is here alone, and he wouldn't dare try to do anything to stop us here. He knows that he'd get into trouble if he did, and I don't

Jane L. Stewart

think he's very brave, even in this new fashion of his unless some of the people he's afraid of are right around to spur him on. You remember how Will Burns thrashed him? He didn't look very brave then, did he?"

"I should say not! All right, I'll tell her and see what she says. Then I'll get back to the boarding-house. You'll go there, won't you?"

"No, I don't think that would be a good idea at all. The best thing for you to do is to wait for me right there in the station. The ticket agent is a woman, and I'm sure she'll let you stay with her until I come, if you get Miss Eleanor to speak to her. Miss Eleanor knows all the people here, and they all like her, and would do anything she asked them to do, if they could.

"And it's easier for me to get to the station without being seen than to the boarding-house. Besides, I think it's right around the station that we'll have the best chance of finding out what they mean to do."

"All right! I'll obey orders," said Dolly. "You're right, too, I think, Bessie."

Jake Hoover, creeping along, was out of sight when Dolly made a swift dash across the street, and in a minute she had disappeared. Bessie knew that Dolly's movements, always rapid, were likely to prove altogether too elusive for Jake's rather slow mind to follow, and, moreover, she was not much afraid of detection, even should Jake catch a glimpse of her chum. Jake was sure that all the Camp Fire Girls were in front of him; he would not, therefore, be looking in the rear for any of them, especially for those he wanted to track down.

Bessie had the harder task. She had to keep herself from Jake's observation until after the train had gone, in any case, and as much longer as possible. As she had told Dolly, she was not very much afraid of anything he might attempt against them, but she saw no use in running any avoidable risks.

Once Jake was out of sight, she made her way slowly toward the station, prepared to make an instant dash for cover should she see Jake returning.

The one thing that was likely to cause him to come back toward her, she figured, was the presence of Holmes or one of the other men who were behind him in the conspiracy, and she was taking the chance, of course, that one of these men was behind her, and a spectator of her movements.

But she could not avoid that. If one of them was there he was, that was all, and she felt that by acting as she had decided to do, she had, at all events, everything to gain and nothing to lose.

The road from the boarding-house to the station was perfectly straight for about three-quarters of a mile, and parallel with the railroad tracks. Then, when the road came to a point opposite the station, it came also to a crossroad, and, about a hundred yards down this crossroad was the station itself.

Bessie reached that point without anything to alarm her or upset her plans, and there she was lucky enough to find a big billboard at the corner, which happened to be a vacant lot. Behind this billboard she took shelter thankfully, feeling sure that it would enable her to see what Jake was doing without any danger of being discovered by him.

Jane L. Stewart

As she had expected, Jake did not enter the station. She had no sooner taken up her position in the shelter of the billboard than she was able to single him out from the men who were lounging about, waiting for the train. His movements were still furtive and sly, and Bessie had to repress a shudder of disgust. Such work seemed to bring out everything small and mean and sly in Jake's nature, and Bessie's thoughts were full of sympathy for his father. After all, Paw Hoover had always been good to her, and when she and Zara had run away from Hedgeville, he had helped them instead of turning them back, as he might so easily have done. It seemed strange to Bessie that so good and kind a man should have such a worthless son.

Twice, as Bessie looked, she saw Jake approach one of the windows of the station building furtively, but each time he was scared away from it before he had a chance to look in.

"Trying to make sure that I'm in there, and afraid of being seen at his spying," decided Bessie. "That's great! If he doesn't see me, he'll just decide that I must be there anyhow, and take a chance. It's a good thing he's such a coward. But I wonder what he thinks we'd do to him, even if we did see him?"

She laughed at the thought. Never having had a really guilty conscience herself, Bessie had no means of knowing what a torturing, weakening thing it is. She could not properly imagine Jake's mental state, in which everything that happened alarmed him. Having done wrong, he fancied all the time that he was about to be haled up, and made to pay for his wrongdoing. And that, of course, was the explanation of his actions, when, as a matter of fact, he could have walked with entire safety into the station and the midst of the Camp Fire Girls.

Soon the whistle of the train that was to carry the Camp Fire Girls to Plum Beach was heard in the distance, and a minute later it roared into the station, stopped, and was off again. Seeing a great waving of handkerchiefs from the last car, Bessie guessed what they meant. Miss Eleanor had agreed to her plan, and this was the way the girls took of bidding her good-bye and good luck.

As soon as the train had gone Jake rushed into the station, and Bessie walked boldly toward it, a new idea in her mind. She had made up her mind that to be afraid of Jake Hoover was a poor policy. If the guess she and Dolly had made concerning his relations with those who were persecuting her was correct, Jake must be a good deal more afraid of them, or of what he had done, than she could possibly be of him, and Bessie knew that there should be no great difficulty in dealing very much as she liked with a coward.

Moreover, the presence of a policeman at the station gave her assurance that she need fear no physical danger from Jake, and she felt that was the only thing that need check her at all.

When she reached the station she looked in the window first, and saw Jake standing by the ticket agent's window. The ticket agent was also the telegraph operator, and Bessie saw that she was writing something on a yellow telegraph blank. Evidently Jake was sending a message, and Bessie knew that, while he could read a very little, Jake had always been so stupid and so lazy that he had never learned to write properly. The sight made her smile, because, unless her plans had miscarried completely, Dolly was inside the little ticket office, and must be hearing every word of that message!

So she waited until Jake, satisfied, turned from the window, and then she walked boldly in. For a minute Jake, who was

100   Jane L. Stewart

looking out of one of the windows in front toward the track, did not see her at all. In that moment Bessie got in line with the ticket window and, seeing Dolly, waved to her to come out. Then she walked over to Jake, smiled at his amazed face as he turned to her, and saluted him cheerfully.

"Hello, Jake Hoover," she said. "Were you looking for me!"

Jake's face fell, and he stared at her in comical dismay.

"Well, I snum!" he said. "How in tarnation did you come to git off that there train, hey?"

"I never was on it, Jake," said Bessie, pleasantly. "You just thought *I* was, you see. You don't want to jump to a conclusion so quickly."

Jake was petrified. When he saw Dolly come out of the ticket office, puzzled by Bessie's action, but entirely willing to back her up, his face turned white.

"You're a pretty poor spy, Jake," said Dolly, contemptuously. "I guess Mr. Holmes won't be very pleased when he gets your message at Canton, telling him Bessie went on that train and then doesn't find her aboard at all."

"What's that?" asked Bessie, suddenly. "Is that the message he sent, Dolly!"

"It certainly is," said Dolly. "Why, what's the matter, Bessie?"

But Bessie didn't answer her. Instead she had raced toward a big railroad map that hung on the wall of the station, and was looking for Canton on it.

"I thought so!" she gasped. Then she ran over to the ticket window, and spoke to the agent.

"If I send a telegram right now, can it be delivered to Miss Mercer, on that train that just went out, before she gets to Canton?" she asked.

The agent looked at her time-table.

"Oh, yes," she said, cheerfully. "That's easy. I'll send it right out for you, and it will reach her at Whitemarsh which is only twenty-five miles away."

"Good!" said Bessie, and wrote out a long telegram. In a minute she returned to Jake and Dolly, and the sound of the ticking telegraph instrument filled the station with its chatter.

"He wanted to run away, Bessie," said Dolly. "But I told him it wasn't polite to do that when a young lady wanted to talk to him, so he stayed. That was nice of him, wasn't it?"

"Very," said Bessie, her tone as sarcastic as Dolly's own. "Now, look here, Jake, what have you done that makes you so afraid of Mr. Holmes and these other wicked men?"

Jake's jaw fell again, but he was speechless. He just stared at her.

"There's no use standing there like a dying calf, Jake Hoover!" said Bessie, angrily. "I know perfectly well you've been up to some dreadful mischief, and these men have told you that if you don't do just as they tell you they'll see that you're punished. Isn't that true?"

"How—how in time did you ever find that out?" stammered Jake.

Jane L. Stewart

"I've known you a long time, Jake Hoover," said Bessie, crisply. "And now tell me this. Haven't I always been willing to be your friend? Didn't I forgive you for all the mean things you did, and help you every way I could? Did I ever tell on you when you'd done anything wrong, and your father would have licked you?"

Bessie's tone grew more kindly as she spoke to him, and Jake seemed to be astonished. He hung his head, and his look at her was sheepish.

"No, I guess you're a pretty good sort, Bessie," he said. "Mebbe I've been pretty mean to you—"

"It's about time you found it out!" said Dolly, furiously. "Oh, I'd like to—"

"Let him alone, Dolly," said Bessie. "I'm running this. Now, Jake, look here. I want to be your friend. I'm very fond of your father, and I'd hate to see him have a lot of sorrow on your account. Don't you know that these men would sacrifice you and throw you over in a minute if they thought they couldn't get anything more out of you? Don't you see that they're just using you, and that when they've got all they can, they'll let you get into any sort of trouble, without lifting a finger to save you?"

"Do you think they'd do that, Bessie? They promised—"

"What are their promises worth, Jake? You ought to know them well enough to understand that they don't care what they do. If you're in trouble, I know someone who will help you. Mr. Jamieson, in the city."

"He—why, he would like to get me into trouble—"

"No, he wouldn't. And if I ask him to help you, I know he'll do it. He can do more for you than they can, too. You go to him, and tell him the whole story, and you'll find he will be a good friend, if you make up your mind to behave yourself after this. We'll forget all the things you've done, and you shall, too, and start over again. Don't you want to be friends, Jake?"

"Sure—sure I do, Bessie!" said Jake, looking really repentant. "Do you mean you'd be willing—that you'd be friends with me, after all the mean things I've done to you?"

Bessie held out her hand.

"I certainly do, Jake," she said. "Now, you go to Mr. Jamieson, and tell him everything you know. Everything, do you hear? I can guess what this latest plot was, but you tell him all you know about it. And you'll find that they've told you a great many things that aren't so at all. Very likely they've just tried to frighten you into thinking you were in danger so that they could make you do what they wanted."

"I'll do it, Bessie!" said Jake.

CHAPTER XI

A NARROW ESCAPE

Despite Dolly's frantic curiosity, Bessie drew Jake aside where there was no danger of their being overheard by any of the others in the station, and talked to him earnestly for a long time. Jake seemed to have changed his whole attitude. He was plainly nervous and frightened, but Dolly could see that he was listening to Bessie with respect. And finally he threw up his head with a gesture entirely strange to him, and, when Bessie held out her hand, shook it happily.

"Here's Mr. Jamieson's address," said Bessie, writing on a piece of paper which she handed to him. "Now you go straight to him, and do whatever he tells you. You'll be all right. How soon will you start?"

"There's a train due right now," said Jake, excitedly. "I'll get aboard, and as soon as I get to town I'll do just as you say, Bessie. Good-bye."

"Good-bye, Jake—and good luck!" said Bessie warmly. "We're going to be good friends, now."

"Well, I never!" gasped Dolly. She stared at Jake's retreating form, and then back to Bessie; as if she were paralyzed with astonishment. "Whatever does this mean, Bessie? I should think you would be pretty hard up for friends before you'd make one of Jake Hoover!"

"Jake's been more stupid than mean, Dolly. And he's found out that he's been wrong, I'm sure. From this time he's going to do a whole lot for us, unless I'm badly mistaken. I'm sure it's better to have him on our side than against us."

"I'm not sure of anything of the sort, Bessie. But do tell me what happened. Why did you send that telegram to Miss Eleanor? And what was in it?"

"I sent it because if I hadn't she would have walked right into a trap—she and Zara. Maybe it was too late, but I hope not. And our staying behind here was a mighty lucky thing. If we hadn't had some warning of what Mr. Holmes and the others were planning, I don't know what would have happened! Zara and I would have been caught, I'm quite sure."

"Don't be so mysterious, Bessie," begged Dolly. "Tell me what you found out, can't you? I'm just as excited and interested as you are, and I should think you would know it, too."

"You'll see it all soon enough, Dolly. Let's find out how soon the next train comes."

"In twenty minutes," said the ticket agent, in answer to the question.

"And is it a through train—an express?" asked Bessie. "Have you a time-table? I'd like to see just where it stops."

She got the time-table, and, after she had examined it carefully, heaved a sigh of relief.

Jane L. Stewart

"The train doesn't stop at any place that isn't marked down for it on the time-table, does it?" she said, as she bought the tickets.

"No, indeed. That's a limited train, and it's almost always on time. They wouldn't stop that except at the regular places for anyone."

"That's all right, then," said Bessie. "Dolly, can't you see the point yet for yourself? Go and look at the map, and if you can't see then, why, I'm not going to tell you! If you're as stupid as all that, you deserve to wait!"

Bessie laughed, but Dolly understood that the laugh was not one of amusement alone, but that Bessie was undergoing a reaction after some strain that had worried her more than she was willing to admit or to show.

"I guess I'm stupid all right," she said, after she had looked at the map. "I don't know what you're driving at, but I suppose you do, and that makes it all right. I'm willing to do whatever you say, but I do like to know why and how things like that are necessary. And I don't think I'm unreasonable, either."

"You're not," said Bessie, suddenly contrite. "But, Dolly dear, I don't want everyone here to know all about us, and the things that are happening to us. You won't mind waiting a little for an explanation, will you?"

"Not when you ask that way," said Dolly, loyally. "But I don't like to have you act as if it were stupid of me not to be able to guess what it is. You wouldn't have known yourself, would you, if Jake Hoover hadn't told you when you two were whispering together?"

"I knew it before that. That's one reason I was able to make

Jake tell me what he did, Dolly. I suppose you don't like my making up with him, either, do you?"

"Oh, no, I don't like it. But that doesn't make any difference. I daresay you've got some very good reason."

"I certainly have, Dolly, and you shall know it soon, too. Listen, there's our train whistling now! We'll start in a minute or two."

"Well, that's good. I hate mysteries. Do you know, Bessie, that if this train only makes one or two stops, we shall be at Plum Beach very soon after Miss Eleanor and the other girls get there!"

"I'm glad of it, Dolly. Tell me, there isn't any station at Plum Beach, is there?"

"No, we'll go to Bay City, and then go back on another train to a little station called Green Cove, and that's within a mile of the beach. It's on a branch railroad that runs along the coast from Bay City."

Then the train came along, and they climbed aboard, happy in having outwitted the enemies of Bessie and Zara. Dolly did not share Bessie's enthusiasm over the conversion of Jake Hoover, though.

"I don't trust him, Bessie," she said. "He may have really meant to turn around and be friends with us, but I don't think he can stick to a promise. I don't know that he means to break them, but he just seems to be helpless. You think he's afraid of Mr. Holmes and those men, don't you?"

"Yes, and he as good as admitted it, too, Dolly."

"Well, what I'm afraid of is that he will see them again, and that he'll do whatever the people he happens to be with tell him."

"I suppose we've got to take that much of a chance, Dolly. We really haven't much choice. My, how this train does go!"

"Why are you looking at your map and your time-table so carefully, Bessie?"

"I want to be sure to know when we're getting near Canton, Dolly. When we do, you must keep your eyes open. You'll see something there that may explain a whole lot of things to you, and make you understand how silly you were not to see through this plot."

Canton was a town of considerable size, and, though the train did not stop there, it slowed down, and ran through the streets and the station at greatly reduced speed. And as the car in which they were sitting went through the station Bessie clutched Dolly's arm, and spoke in her ear.

"Look!" she said. "There on the platform! Did you ever see those men before!"

Dolly gave a startled cry as her eyes followed Bessie's pointing finger.

"Mr. Holmes!" she exclaimed. "And that's that little lawyer, Mr. Brack. And the old man with the whiskers—"

"Is Farmer Weeks, of course! Do you see the fourth man standing with them? See how he pushes his coat back! He's a constable and he's so proud of it he wants everyone to see his badge!"

"Bessie! Do you mean they were waiting here for you?"

"For me and Zara, Dolly! If I had been on a train that stopped here—but I wasn't! And I guess Miss Eleanor must have got my telegram in time to hide Zara so that they didn't find her on the other train, too, or else we'd see something of her."

Dolly laughed happily. Then she did a reckless thing, showing herself at the window, and shaking her fist defiantly as the car, with rapidly gathering speed, passed the disconsolate group on the station platform. Holmes was the first to see her, and his face darkened with a swift scowl. Then he caught sight of Bessie, and, seizing Brack's arm, pointed the two girls out to him, too. But there was nothing whatever to be done.

The train, after slowing down, was already beginning to move fast again, and there was no way in which it could be stopped, or in which the group of angry men on the platform could board it. They could only stand in powerless rage, and look after it. Bessie and Dolly, of course, could not hear the furious comments that Holmes was making as he turned angrily to old Weeks. But they could make a guess, and Dolly turned an elfin face, full of mischievous delight, to Bessie.

"That's one time they got fooled," she exclaimed.

"I'm sorry they found out we were on this train, though," said Bessie, gravely, "It means that we'll have trouble with them after we get to Plum Beach, I'm afraid."

"Who cares?" said Dolly. "If they can't do any better there than they've done so far on this trip, we needn't worry much, I guess."

Jane L. Stewart

"Well, do you see what they were up to, now, Dolly?"

Dolly wrinkled her brows.

"I guess so," she said. "They meant to come aboard the train at Canton and try to get hold of you and Zara. But I don't see why—"

"Why they should pick out Canton rather than any other station where the trains stop along the line?"

"That's just it, Bessie. Why should they?"

"That's the whole point, Dolly. Look at this map. Do you see the state boundaries? For just a little way this line is in the state Canton is in—and Canton is in the same state as Hedgeville!"

"Oh!" gasped Dolly. "You were right, Bessie, I *was stupid*! I might have thought of that! That's why they had Jake there, and what his telegram was. But how clever of you to think of it! How did you ever guess it?"

"I just happened to think that if we did go into that state, it would be easy for them to get hold of Zara and me, if they only knew about it beforehand. Because, you see, in that state Farmer Weeks is legal guardian for both of us, and he could make us come with him if he caught us there."

"Well, I think it was mighty clever of you. Of course, when you had the idea, it was easy to see it, once you had the map so that you could make sure. But I never would have thought of it, so I couldn't have looked it up to make sure, because I wouldn't have thought there was anything to look up."

"What I'm wondering," said Bessie, "is what Miss Eleanor

did to keep them from getting Zara. If you ask me, that's the really clever thing that's been done to-day. I was dreadfully frightened when I decided that was what they were up to."

"Well, your telegram helped," said Dolly. "If it hadn't been for that, they'd have been taken completely by surprise. Just imagine how they would have felt, if they'd looked up when their train stopped at Canton, and had seen Farmer Weeks coming down the aisle."

"It would have been dreadful, wouldn't it, Bessie? Do you know, Miss Eleanor wasn't a bit anxious to have us stay behind? She was afraid something would happen, I believe. But it's certainly a good thing that you thought of doing it, and had your way."

"I was afraid they'd try to play some sort of a trick, Dolly. That's why I wanted to wait. I couldn't tell what it would be, but I knew that if Jake was there it wouldn't do any harm to watch him and see what he did. I didn't expect to get him on our side, though. Before I talked to him, of course, I was really only guessing, but he told me all he knew about the plan. They hadn't told him everything, but with what I had guessed it was enough."

"No one trusts him, you see, Bessie. It's just as I said."

"Well, do you know, I shouldn't wonder if that was one reason for his being so untrustworthy, Dolly. Maybe if he finds that we are going to trust him, it will change him, and make him act very differently."

"I certainly hope so, Bessie, but I'm afraid of him. I'm afraid that they will find out what we've done, and try to use him to trick us, now that we think he's on our side."

Jane L. Stewart

"We'll have to look out for that, Dolly, of course. But I don't believe he's as black as he's painted. He must have some good qualities. Perhaps they'll begin to come out now."

At Bay City, where they arrived comparatively early in the afternoon, they had a surprise, for Miss Eleanor and all the girls were at the station to meet them, including Zara, who looked nervous and frightened.

"Oh, I'm so glad you've come here safely, Bessie," said Eleanor, flinging her arms about Bessie's neck. "Your train came right through, didn't it?"

"Yes, and we saw Mr. Holmes and the rest of them on the platform at Canton," said Bessie, laughing. "Did they get aboard your train?"

"Did they?" cried Eleanor. "They most certainly did, and when they couldn't find either you or Zara, they were so angry that I was afraid they were going to burst! I don't believe I ever saw men so dreadfully disappointed in my life."

"How did you manage to hide Zara?"

"That was awfully funny, Bessie. I found some friends of mine were on the train, travelling in a private car. As soon as I got your telegram, I went back to see them. They had a boy with them, who is just about Zara's size. So Zara dressed up in a suit of his clothes, and she was sitting in their car, with him, when they came aboard to look for her."

"Did they look in that car?"

"Yes. They had a warrant, or something, so they had a right to go everywhere on the train—and they did!"

"I should think the people who didn't have anything to do with us must have been furious."

"Oh, they were, but it didn't do them any good. They searched through the whole train, but Zara looked so different in boy's clothes that they never even seemed to suspect her at all. She kept perfectly still, you see, and after they had held us up for nearly an hour, we came on."

"Oh, how mad they must have been!"

"You ought to have seen them! It made us very late getting here, of course, and we missed the train we were to take to Green Cove. But I think we would have waited here, anyhow, until you came. I was very anxious about you, Bessie. What a clever trick that was! If it hadn't been for you, we would have been caught without a chance to do anything at all."

"Bessie's made friends with Jake Hoover, too," said Dolly, disgustedly. "Tell Miss Eleanor about that, Bessie."

"You did exactly the right thing," said Eleanor, when she had heard the story, much to Dolly's disgust. "I agree with Dolly that we will have to look out for him, just the same, but there is a chance that he may do what he promised. Anyhow, there's a lot to gain and very little to lose."

CHAPTER XII

PLUM BEACH

On the way to Plum Beach, on the little branch line that carried the girls from Bay City to Green Cove, Eleanor was very thoughtful, and Bessie and Dolly were kept busy in telling the other girls of their experiences. They wanted to hear from Zara, too, just how she had escaped.

"I don't see how you kept your face straight," said Dolly. "I know I would have burst right out laughing, Zara."

"You wouldn't think so if you knew Farmer Weeks," said Zara, making a wry face. "I can tell you I didn't want to laugh, Dolly. Why, he was within a few feet of me, and looking straight at me! I was sure he'd guess that it was I."

"He always looks at everyone that way—just as if they owed him money," said Bessie. "Nasty old man! I don't blame you for being nervous, Zara."

"Oh, neither do I," said Dolly. "But it was funny to think of his being so near you and having no idea of it. That's what would have made me laugh."

"It seems funny enough, now," admitted Zara, with a smile.

"But, you see, I was perfectly certain that he did have a very good idea of where I was. I was expecting him to take hold of me any moment, and tell the constable to take me off the train."

"I wonder how long this sort of thing is going to keep up," said Margery Burton, angrily. "Until you two girls are twenty-one?"

"I hope not," laughed Bessie, and then she went on, more seriously, "I really do think that if Jake Hoover sticks to what he said, and takes our side, Mr. Jamieson is likely to find out something that will give him a chance to settle matters. You see, we've been fighting in the dark so far."

"I don't see that we've been fighting at all, yet," said Margery. "They keep on trying to do something, and we manage to keep them from doing it. That's not my idea of a fight. I wish we could do some of the hitting ourselves."

"So do I, Margery. And that's just what I think we may be able to do now, if we have Jake on our side. He must know something about what they've been doing. They couldn't keep him from finding out, it seems to me."

"But will he tell? That seems to be the question."

"Yes, that's it, exactly. Well, if he does, then we'll know why they're doing all this. You see, Mr. Jamieson can't figure on what they're going to do next, or how to beat them at their own game, simply because he doesn't know what their game is. They know just what they want to do, while we haven't any idea, except that they're anxious to have Zara and myself back where Farmer Weeks can do as he likes with us."

"Well, it would be fine to be able to beat them, Bessie, but

Jane L. Stewart

right now I'm more worried about what they will try to do next. This is a pretty lonely place we're going to, and they're so bold that there's no telling what they may try next."

"That's so—and they know we're coming here, too. Jake told them that."

"They would probably have found it out anyhow," said Dolly. "And there's one thing—he didn't try to warn them that you knew about what they meant to do at Canton, Bessie."

"No, he didn't. And he could have done it very easily, too. Oh, I think we can count on Jake now, all right. He's pretty badly frightened, and he's worried about himself. He'll stick to the side that seems the most likely to help him. All I hope is that he will go to see Mr. Jamieson."

"Do you think he will?"

"Why not? Even if they get hold of him again, I think there will be time enough for him to see Mr. Jamieson first. And I've got an idea that Mr. Jamieson will be able to scare him pretty badly."

"All out for Green Cove," called the conductor just then, appearing in the doorway, and there was a rush for the end of the car.

"Well, here we are," said Eleanor. "This isn't much of a city, is it?"

It was not. Two or three bungalows and seashore cottages were in sight, but most of the traffic for the Green Cove station came from scattered settlements along the coast. It was a region where people liked to live alone, and they were willing to be some distance from the railroad to secure the isolation that appealed to them. A little pier poked its nose out into the waters of the cove, and beside this pier was a gasoline launch, battered and worn, but amply able, as was soon proved, to carry all the girls and their belongings at a single load.

"Thought you wasn't coming," said the old sailor who owned the launch, as he helped them to get settled aboard.

"We missed the first connecting train and had to wait, Mr. Salters," said Eleanor. "I hope you didn't sell the fish and clams you promised us to someone else?"

"No, indeed," said old Salters. "They're waitin' for you at the camp, ma'am, and I fixed up the place, too, all shipshape. The tents is all ready, though why anyone should sleep in such contraptions when they can have a comfortable house is more'n I can guess."

"Each to his taste, you know," laughed Eleanor. "I suppose we'll be able to get you to take us out in the launch sometimes while we're here?"

"Right, ma'am! As often as you like," he answered. "My old boat here ain't fashionable enough for some of the folk, but she's seaworthy, and she won't get stuck a mile an' a half from nowhere, the way Harry Semmes and that new fangled boat of his done the other day when he had a load of young ladies aboard."

He chuckled at the recollection. But while he had been talking he had not been idle, and the *Sally S.*, as his launch was called, had been making slow but steady progress until she was outside the cove and headed north. Soon, too, he ran her inside the protecting spot of land of which Dolly had

Jane L. Stewart

spoken to Bessie, and they were in such smooth water that, even had any of them had any tendency toward seasickness, there would have been no excuse for it.

In half an hour he stopped the engine, and cast his anchor overboard. He wore no shoes and stockings, and now, rolling up his trousers, he jumped overboard.

"Hand me the dunnage first," he said. "I'll get that ashore, and then I'll take the rest of you, one at a time."

"Indeed you won't," laughed Eleanor. "We're not afraid of getting our feet wet. Come on, girls, it's only two feet deep! Roll up your skirts and take off your shoes and stockings, and we'll wade ashore."

She set the example, and in a very short time they were all safely ashore, with much laughter at the splashing that was involved.

"Mr. Salters could run the *Sally S.* ashore, but it would be a lot of trouble to get her afloat again, and this is the way we always do here. It's lots of fun really," Eleanor explained.

Soon they were all ashore, and inspecting the camp which had been laid out in preparation for them.

"Real army tents, with regular floors and cots, these are," said Eleanor. "Sleeping on the ground wouldn't be very wise here. And there's no use taking chances. I'm responsible to the mothers and fathers of all you girls, after all, and I'm bound to see that you go home better than when you started, instead of worse."

"I think they're fine," said Margery. "Oh, I do love the seashore! How long shall we stay, Miss Eleanor!"

"I don't know," said the Guardian, a shade of doubt darkening her eyes. "You know, Margery"—she spoke in a low tone—"that seems to depend partly on things we can't really control. There seems to me to be something really quite desperate about the way Mr. Holmes and his friends are going for Bessie and Zara.

"Maybe they will make trouble for us here. It *is* rather isolated, you know, and I can't help remembering that we're on the coast, and that a few miles away the coast is that of Bessie's state—the state she mustn't be in."

"That's so," said Margery, gravely. "You mean that if they managed to get hold of Bessie or Zara, and took them out to sea and then landed them in that state they'd be able to hold them there?"

"It worries me, Margery. The trouble is, you see, that once they're in that state, it doesn't matter how they were taken there, but they can be held. If Zara's father gets free, why, he would be able to get her back, I suppose. Mr. Jamieson says so. But there's no one with a better right to Bessie, so far as we know. I'm really more worried about her than about Zara."

"We'll all be careful," promised Margery, with fire in her eye. "And I guess they'll have to be pretty smart to find any way of getting her away from us. I'll talk to the girls, and I'll try to be watching myself all the time."

"I'm hungry," announced Dolly. "Just as hungry as a bear! Can't we have supper pretty soon, Miss Eleanor!"

"Supper?" scoffed Miss Eleanor. "Why, we haven't had our dinner yet! But we'll have that just as soon as it's cooked. I've just been waiting for someone to say they were hungry.

Jane L. Stewart

Dolly, you're elected cook. Since you're the hungry one, you can cook the dinner."

"I certainly will! I'll get it all the sooner that way. May I pick out who's to help me, Miss Eleanor?"

"That's the rule. You certainly can."

"Then I pick out all the girls," announced Dolly. "Every one of you—and no shirking, mind!'"

She laughed merrily, and in a moment she had set every girl to some task. Even Margery obeyed her orders cheerfully, for the rule was there, and, even though Dolly had twisted it a bit, it was recognized as a good joke. Moreover, everyone was hungry and wanted the meal to be ready as soon as possible.

"There's good water at the top of that path," said Eleanor, pointing to a path that led up a bluff that backed against the tents. "I think maybe we'll build a wooden pipe-line to bring the water right down here, but for to-day we'll have to carry it from the spring there."

"Is there driftwood here for a camp fire, do you suppose, the way there was last year, Miss Eleanor?" asked one of the other girls. "I'll never forget the lovely fires we had then!"

"There's lots of it, I'm afraid," said Eleanor, gravely.

"Why are you 'afraid'?" asked Bessie, wonderingly.

"Because all the driftwood, or most of it, comes from wrecked ships, Bessie. This beach looks calm and peaceful now, but in the winter, when the great northeast storms blow, this is a terrible coast, and lots and lots of ships are wrecked.

Men are drowned very often, too."

"Oh, I never thought of that!"

"Still, some of the wood is just lost from lumber schooners that are loaded too heavily," said Eleanor. "And it certainly does make a beautiful fire, all red and green and blue, and oh, all sorts of colors and shades you never even dreamed of! We'll have a ceremonial camp fire while we're here, and it is certainly true that there is no fire half so beautiful as that we get when we use the wood that the sea casts up."

"Don't they often find lots of other things beside wood along the coast after a great storm, Miss Eleanor!"

"Yes, indeed! There are people who make their living that way. Wreckers, they call them, you know. Of course, it isn't as common to find really valuable things now as it was in the old days."

"Why not? I thought more things were carried at sea than ever," said Dolly.

"There aren't so many wrecks, Dolly, for one thing. And then, in the old days, before steam, and the great big ships they have now, even the most valuable cargoes were carried in wooden ships that were at the mercy of these great storms."

"Oh, and now they send those things in the big ships that are safer, I suppose?"

"Yes. You very seldom hear of an Atlantic liner being wrecked, you know. It does happen once in a great while, of course, but they are much more likely to reach the port they sail for than the old wooden ships. In the old days many and

Jane L. Stewart

many a ship sailed that was never heard of, but you could count the ships that have done that in the last few years on the fingers of one hand."

"But there was a frightful wreck not so very long ago, wasn't there? The Titanic?"

"Yes. That was the most terrible disaster since men have gone to sea at all. You see, she was so much bigger, and could carry so many more people than the old ships, that, when she did go down, it was naturally much worse. But the wreckers never made any profit out of her. She went down in the middle of the ocean, and no one will ever see her again."

"Couldn't divers go down after her?"

"No. She was too deep for that. Divers can only go down a certain distance, because, below that, the pressure is too great, and they wouldn't live."

"Stop talking and attend to your dinner, Dolly," said Margery, suddenly. "You pretended you were hungry, and now you're so busy talking that you're forgetting about the rest of us. We're hungry, too. Just remember that!"

"I can talk and work at the same time," said Dolly. "Is everything ready? Because, if it is, so is dinner. Come on, girls! The clams first. I've cooked it—I'm not going to put it on the table, too."

"No, we ought to be glad to get any work out of her at all," laughed Margery, as she carried the steaming, savory clams to the table. "I suppose every time we want her to do some work the rest of the time we're here, she'll tell us about this dinner."

"I won't have to," boasted Dolly. "You'll all remember it. All I'm afraid of is that you won't be satisfied with the way anyone else cooks after this. I've let myself out this time!"

It *was* a good dinner—a better dinner than anyone had thought Dolly could cook. But, despite her jesting ways, Dolly was a close observer, and she had not watched Margery, a real genius in the art of cooking, in vain. Everyone enjoyed it, and, when they had eaten all they could, Dolly lay back in the sand with Bessie.

"Well, wasn't I right? Don't you love this place?" she asked.

"I certainly think I do," said Bessie. "It's so peaceful and quiet. I didn't believe any place could be as calm as the mountains, but I really think this is."

"I love to hear the surf outside, too," said Dolly. "It's as if it were singing a lullaby. I think the surf, and the sighing of the wind in the trees is the best music there is."

"Those noises were the real beginning of music, Dolly," said Eleanor. "Did you know that? The very first music that was ever written was an attempt to imitate those songs of nature."

After the dishes were washed and put away, everyone sat on the beach, watching the sky darken. First one star and then another came out, and the scene was one of idyllic beauty. And then, as if to complete it, a yacht appeared, small, but beautiful and graceful, steaming toward them. Its sides were lighted, and from its deck came the music of a violin, beautifully played.

"Oh, how lovely that is!" said Eleanor. "Why, look! I do

believe it is going to anchor!"

And, sure enough, the noise of the anchor chains came over the water.

CHAPTER XIII

THE MYSTERIOUS YACHT

But, beautiful as the yacht undoubtedly was, the sight of it and the sound of the slipping anchor chains brought a look of perplexity and even of distress to Eleanor's eyes.

"That's very curious," she said, thoughtfully. "There are no cottages or bungalows near here. Those people can't be coming here just for a visit, or they would take another anchorage. And it's a strange thing for them to choose this cove if they are just cruising along the coast."

"There weren't any yachts here last year when we were camping," said Margery. "But it is a lovely spot, and it's public land along here, isn't it?"

"No, not exactly. It won't be used for a long time, I expect, but it has an owner. An old gentleman in Bay City owns all the shore front along here for half a mile, and he has been holding on to it with the idea that it would get more valuable as time went on. Probably it will, too."

"Well, he lets people come here to camp, doesn't he?"

"Oh, yes. He's glad to have people here, I think, because he

Jane L. Stewart

thinks that if they see how lovely it is, they will want to buy the land. I suppose perhaps these people on the yacht have permission from him to come here, just as we have. But I do wish they had waited until we had gone, or else that they had come and gone before we got here at all."

"Perhaps they will just stay for the night," said Margery. "I should think that a small boat like that would be very likely to put in overnight, and do its sailing in the daytime. Probably the people on board of her aren't in a hurry, and like to take things easily."

"Well, we won't find out anything about her to-night, I imagine," said Eleanor. "In the morning we'll probably learn what their plans are, and then it will be time to make any changes that are necessary in our own arrangements."

"Do you mean you wouldn't stay here if they did, Miss Eleanor?"

"I won't say that, Margery. We don't know who they are yet. They may be very nice people—there's no way of telling to-night. But if they turn out to be undesirable, we can move quite easily, I think. There are plenty of other beaches nearby where we'll be just as comfortable as we are here."

"Oh, but I don't believe any of them are as beautiful as this one, Miss Eleanor."

"Neither do I, Margery. Still, we can't always pick and choose the things we do, or always do what pleases us best."

On the yacht everything seemed to be quiet. When the anchor had gone down, the violin playing ceased, and, though the girls strained their ears to listen, there was no sound of conversation, such as might reasonably have been expected to come across the quiet water. Still there was nothing strange about that. It might well be that everyone on board was below, eating supper, and in that case voices would probably not come to them.

"I'd like to own that yacht," said Dolly, gazing at her enviously. "What a lot of fun you could have with her, Bessie! Think of all the places one could see. And you wouldn't have to leave a place until you got ready. Steamers leave port just as railroad trains pull out of a station, and you may have to go away when you haven't half finished seeing all the things you want to look at."

"Maybe they'll send a boat ashore soon," said Margery, hopefully. "I certainly would like to see the sort of people who are on board."

"So would I," said Eleanor, but with a different and a more anxious meaning in her tone.

"I wish that man with the violin would start playing again," said Dolly. "I love to hear him, and it seems to me it's especially beautiful when the sound comes to you over the water that way."

"Music always sounds best over the water," said Eleanor. "He does play well. I've been to concerts, and heard famous violin players who didn't play a bit better—or as well, some of them."

And just at that moment the music came to them again, wailing, mournful, as if the strings of the violin were sobbing under the touch of the bow, held in the fingers of a real master. The music blended with the night, and the listening girls seemed to lose all desire to talk, so completely did they fall under the spell of the player.

But after a little while a harsh voice on the deck of the yacht interrupted the musician. They could not distinguish the words, but the speaker was evidently annoyed by the music, for it stopped, and then, for a few minutes, there was an argument in which the voices of two men rose shrilly.

"Well, I guess the concert is over," said Dolly, getting up. "Who wants a drink? I'm thirsty."

"So am I!" came in chorus from half a dozen of those who were sitting on the sands.

"Serve you right if you all had to go after your own water," said Dolly. "But I'm feeling nice to-night. I guess it's the music. Come on, Bessie—feel like taking a little walk with me?"

"I don't mind," said Bessie, rising, and stretching her arms luxuriously. "Where are you going?"

"Up the bluff first, to get a pail of water from that spring. After that—well, we'll see."

"Just like Jack and Jill," said Bessie, as they trudged up the path, carrying a pail between them.

"I hope we won't be like them and fall down," said Dolly. "I suppose I'd be Jack—and I don't want to break my crown."

"It's an easy path. I guess we're safe enough," said Bessie. "It really hardly seems worth while to fix up that pipe-line Miss Eleanor spoke about."

"Oh, you'll find it's worth while, Bessie. The salt air makes everyone terribly thirsty, and after you've climbed this path a few times it won't seem so easy to be running up and down all the time. There are so many other things to do here that it's a pity to waste time doing the same thing over and over again when you don't really need to."

"I suppose that's so, too. It's always foolish to do work that you don't need to do—I mean that can be done in some easier way. If your time's worth anything at all, you can find some better use for it."

"That's what I say! It would be foolish and wasteful to set a hundred men to digging when one steam shovel will do the work better and quicker than they can. And it's the same way with this water here. If we can put up a pipe in about an hour that will save two or three hours of chasing every day, whenever water is needed, it must be sensible to do it."

They got the water down without any mishap, however, and it was eagerly welcomed.

"It's good water," said Margery. "But not as good as the water at Long Lake and in the mountains."

"That's the best water in the world, Margery," said Eleanor. "This is cold, though, and it's perfectly healthy. And, after all, that is as much as we can expect. Are you and Bessie going for a walk, Dolly?"

"We thought we would, if you don't mind."

"I don't mind, of course. But don't go very far. Stay near enough so that you can hear if we call, or for us to hear you if you should happen to call to us."

Dolly looked startled.

"Why, should we want to call you?" she asked.

"No reason that I can think of now, Dolly. But—well, I suppose I'm nervous. The way they tried to get hold of Bessie and Zara at Canton to-day makes me feel that we've got to be very careful. And there is no use taking unnecessary chances."

"All right," said Dolly, with a laugh. "But I guess we're safe enough to-night, anyhow. They haven't had time to find out yet how Bessie fooled them. My, but they'll be mad when they do find out what happened!"

"They certainly will," laughed Margery. "I wouldn't want to be in Jake Hoover's shoes."

"I hope nothing will happen to him," said Eleanor, anxiously. "It would be a great pity for him to get into trouble now."

"I think he deserves to get into some sort of trouble," said Dolly, stoutly. "He's made enough for other people."

"That's true enough, Dolly. But it wouldn't do us any good if he got into trouble now, you know."

"No, but it might do him some good—the brute! You haven't seen him when he was cutting up, the way I have, Miss Eleanor."

"No, and I'm glad I didn't. But you say it might do him some good. That's just what I think it would not do. He has just made up his mind to be better, and suppose he sees that, as a reward, he gets himself into trouble. What is he likely to do, do you think?"

"That's so," said Margery. "You're going off without thinking again, Dolly, as usual. He'd cut loose altogether, and think there wasn't any sort of use in being decent."

"Well, I haven't much faith in his having reformed," said Dolly. "It may be that he has, but it seems too good to be true to me. I bet you'll find that he'll be on their side, after all, and that he'll just spend his time thinking up some excuse for having put them on the wrong track to-day."

"I think that's likely to keep him pretty busy, Dolly," said Eleanor, dryly. "And that's one reason I really am inclined to believe that he'll change sides, and go to Charlie Jamieson, as Bessie advised him to do."

"Well, if he does, it won't be because he's sorry, but because he's afraid," said Dolly. "If he can be of any use to us, why, I hope he's all right. I don't like him, and I never will like him, and there isn't any use in pretending about it!"

Everyone laughed at that.

"You're quite right, Dolly," said Margery. "When you dislike a person anyone who can see you or hear you knows about it. I'll say that for you—you don't pretend to be friends with people when you really hate them."

"Why should I? Come on, Bessie, if we're going for a walk. If we stay here much longer Margery'll get so dry from talking that we'll have to go and get her some more water."

"Let's go up the path and get on the bluff again," said Bessie. "I like it up there, because you seem to be able to see further out to sea than you can here."

"All right. I don't care where we go, anyhow, and it is more interesting up there than on the beach, I think."

The night was a beautiful one, and walking was really delightful. Below them the beach stretched, white and smooth, as far as the cove itself. At each end of the cove the bluff on which they were walking curved and turned toward the sea, stretching out to form two points of land that enclosed the cove.

"They say this would be a perfect harbor if there was a bigger channel dredged in," said Dolly. "Of course it's very small, but I guess it was used in the old days. There are all sorts of stories about buried treasure being hidden around here."

"Do you believe those stories, Dolly?"

"Not I! If there was any treasure around here it would have been found ever so long ago. They're just stories. I guess those pirates spent most of the money they stole, and I guess they didn't get half as much as people like to pretend, anyhow."

"It would be fun to find something like that, though, Dolly."

"Well, Bessie King, you're the last person I would ever have expected even to think of anything so silly! You'd better get any nonsense of that sort out of your head right away. There's nothing in those old stories."

"I suppose not," said Bessie, and sighed. "But in a place like this it doesn't seem half so hard to believe that it's possible, somehow. It looks like just the sort of place for romance and adventure. But—oh, well, I guess I'm just moonstruck. Dolly, look at that!"

Her eyes had wandered suddenly toward the yacht, and now, from their higher elevation, they were able to see a small boat drawing away from her, on the seaward side, and so out of sight of the girls on the beach.

"That's funny," said Dolly, puzzled. "I should think that if they were going to send a boat ashore she'd come straight in."

"Let's watch and see what happens, Dolly."

"You bet we will! I wouldn't go now until I knew what they were up to for anything!"

"It's going straight out to sea, Dolly, and it's keeping so that the yacht is between it and the shore. It does look as if they didn't want to be seen, doesn't it!"

"It certainly does! Look, there it goes through the little gap in the bar! See? Now it will be hidden from the people on shore—and it's going toward West Point, too. See, I'll bet they're going to make a landing there!"

They hurried along the bluff, and in a few minutes they saw the boat graze the beach at the end of West Point. Three men jumped out and hauled the little craft up on the shore, and then they began to move inland, toward Bessie and Dolly.

"We'd better work back toward the camp," said Dolly, excitedly. "It wouldn't do to have them see us—not until we know more about them."

"I wonder if they'll come back this way, toward the camp? And why do you suppose they're acting that way? It seems very funny to me."

"It does to me, too. I'm beginning to think Miss Eleanor had a good reason for being nervous, Bessie. I don't believe that yacht is here for any good purpose."

"It's a good thing we came up this way, isn't it?"

"It certainly is, if we can manage to find out something about them. I say, do you remember where the spring is? Well, right by it there's a mound, with a whole lot of bushes. I believe we could hide there, and be waiting as they come along."

"Let's try it, anyhow. Maybe there's something we ought to know."

They found it easy to hide themselves, and when, a few minutes later, the three men came along, they were secure from observation.

"Do you think it's Mr. Holmes?" whispered Bessie, voicing the thought both of them had had.

"It's just as likely as not! It's the sneaky way he would act," said Dolly, viciously. "They're pretty careful about the way they walk—see?"

But then the men came into the range of their eyes, and the sigh of disappointment that rose from them was explained by Dolly's disgusted, "It's not Mr. Holmes, or anyone else I ever saw before."

The men came nearer, and seemed to be looking down at the camp.

"They're the ones! That's the outfit, all right," said one of them. "Well, it's easy to keep an eye on them."

CHAPTER XIV

A NIGHT ALARM

Bessie and Dolly looked at one another. Holmes wasn't there, but who but Holmes or someone working for him could have any such sinister interest in keeping an eye on the camp as was implied by that sly remark? Evidently luck had favored them once more, and they had stumbled again on early evidence of another coming attack.

But they took little time—could take little time, indeed—to think of the meaning of what they had heard. It was too important for them to find out as much as possible from these men. They dared not speak to one another; the men were so close that they were almost afraid that the sound of their own breathing would betray them.

And, dark as it was, they could see that these were men of a type who would stop at little if they felt they were in danger of failure. They were big, burly, ugly-looking men, rough in speech and manner, and, though they masked their movements, and went about their business, whatever it might be, as quietly as possible, their quietness furtive and assumed and by no means natural to them.

"They won't run away to-night, Jeff," grumbled one of the

men. "You ain't a-goin' to stay here and watch them, are you?"

"No, I'm not—but you are," growled the one addressed as Jeff. "See here, my buck, the boss don't want any slip-up on this job—see? He's been stung once too often. I'm goin' back to the boat, but you and Tim will stay here till daylight—right here, mind you!"

"Aw, shucks, that's a fine job to give us!" growled Tim. "Larry's got the right dope, Jeff. They won't run away to-night."

"Listen here—who's giving orders here? What I say goes—do you get that? If you don't, I'll find a way to make you, and pretty quick, too. I don't want none of your lip, Tim."

"What's the game, Jeff?" asked the man Larry, in milder tones. "We'll do as you say, all right, all right, but can't you tell a guy what's doin'?"

"I don't know myself, boys, and that's a fact," said Jeff, seemingly mollified by this submission to his orders. "But the boss wants them two gals—and what he wants he gits, sooner or later."

"Guess he does!" laughed Tim. "You said something that time, Jeff!"

"There's money in it, I know that," Jeff went on. "Big money—though I'm blowed if I see where! But we'll get our share if we do our part."

"I can use any that comes my way, all right," said Larry, with a smothered laugh. "Always broke—that's what I am!"

"How about the morning, Jeff?" asked Tim. "We can't stay here when it gets to be light. They'd spot us in a minute."

"Won't be any need then, Tim. We can keep an eye on them from the yacht. And the boss is apt to turn up here himself most any time."

"Why not pull it off to-night, Jeff?" asked Larry. "It's a good chance, I'd say."

"Ain't got my orders yet, Larry. As soon as the boss turns up there'll be plenty doing. Keep an eye out for a red light from the deck. That'll be a sign to watch out for anything that comes along. We may show it—we may not. But if we do, be lively."

"All right," growled Tim. "But let's quit this nursemaid job as soon as we can, Jeff. We're good pals of yours—and this ain't no game for a grown man, you know that."

"'Twon't be so bad," said Jeff, comfortingly. "Nights ain't so long—and you can take turns sleeping. It's all right as long as one of you stays awake."

"So long, Jeff," said both the men who were to stay behind, then, in unison.

"Good-night," answered Jeff. "I'll have a boat at the point for you at daylight. Good luck!"

And he went off, quietly, walking easily, so that the noise of his footsteps would not reach those on the beach below.

From the beach the voices of the girls rose faintly. Words could not be distinguished, but Bessie and Dolly could both guess that their prolonged absence must be beginning to give

Miss Eleanor and the others some uneasiness.

They were trapped, however, although they were in no real danger. The men who had been left on guard were between them and the path; they could not possibly pass them without arousing them, and they did not care to take the chance of making a wild dash for freedom unless it became absolutely necessary.

Bessie weighed the chances. It seemed likely to her that she and Dolly, taking the two men by surprise, could slip by them and reach the beach safely. But if they did that, the men would know that their plans were known, and that their talk had been overheard, and that would be to throw away half of the advantage they had gained. It would be better a thousand times, Bessie felt, to wait, and take the faint chance that both men might go to sleep together, and so give them the chance to escape unseen.

For some minutes the silence was unbroken save for the faint murmur of the voices from the beach. Then Larry spoke to his companion.

"Say, Tim, don't think much of this game, do you?" he said.

"Sure don't!" grunted Tim. "Just like Jeff, though. Takes the easy lay himself and don't care what he puts up to us."

"Got any money?"

"About five dollars. Why? Want to borrow it? Just as soon you had it as me! Can't spend it here, anyhow."

"No. Wouldn't do me any good. Got lots of my own out on the yacht."

"Wish there was a place near here where I could get a drink. Seems like I was choking to death."

"Lots of water right by you," said Larry, with a hoarse laugh. "Help yourself—it's free!"

"Water—pah!" snorted Tim. "That's not what I want, and you know it, Larry."

"Say, come to think of it, there's an elegant little roadhouse a ways back in the country here, Tim. About half an hour there and back, I judge."

Tim grunted uneasily.

"Think it's safe?" he queried. "If Jeff got on to us—"

"Shucks! What could he do? We ain't his hired hands."

"The boss, though—suppose Jeff told him?"

"He wouldn't, and how's he goin' to find out, anyhow? Nothin's goin' to happen to-night, you can bet on that. Come on, be a sport, Tim! We've got as much on Jeff as he's got on us, if it comes down to that, ain't we?"

"I dunno. I'm kind of leery, when he told us to stick, Larry."

"I thought you had more nerve, Tim. Didn't ever think you'd stand for no game like this. But, if you're afraid—"

"Come on!" said Tim, angrily. "I'll show you if I'm afraid! I guess it's safe enough."

"That's more like my old pal Tim. I knew you had nerve enough. Let's be movin'. The sooner we go, the sooner we'll be back. And we'll show who's afraid—eh, old sport?"

"That's the stuff, Larry! Guess there ain't no one big enough to tell us what to do."

And, with linked arms, they moved off. Bessie and Dolly, hardly able to believe in the good luck that left the way to the beach clear, held their breath for a moment. Then Bessie, seeing that Dolly was about to rise, whispered to her.

"Not yet, Dolly," she said, tensely. "Wait till we're sure they can't see us. No use taking chances now."

"All right, Bessie, but what luck! I was afraid we'd have to stay here until daylight, and I was wondering what Miss Eleanor and the girls would think!"

"So was I. I'm afraid they're worried about us already. But it wasn't our fault, and it really is a good thing we heard them, isn't it? The 'boss' they're talking about must be Mr. Holmes, don't you think!"

"I don't see who else it could possibly be. Come on, Bessie. I think it's time now, they're out of sight."

Slowly and carefully, to take into account the off chance that Jeff, the other man, might have come back to see if his sentinels were faithful, they slipped across the path and made their way down. And at the bottom, as they reached the beach, Eleanor Mercer spied them, with a glad cry.

"Oh, whatever kept you so long?" she exclaimed. "How glad I am to see you back safely! We couldn't imagine what on earth was keeping you."

"You shouldn't have stayed so long," said Margery Burton.

"We were just going to start out to look for you."

"You wouldn't have had very far to go. We've been right at the top of the path for three-quarters of an hour," said Dolly, excitedly.

"It wasn't our fault, really! We couldn't get here any sooner," said Bessie. "You see—"

And, quietly, being less excited and hysterical than Dolly, she explained what they had discovered, and the trap in which they had allowed themselves to be caught.

"We thought it was better to wait there than to let them know we had heard them," she ended. "You see, they think now that we haven't any suspicions at all, and that we'll be off our guard. Don't you suppose Mr. Holmes must be coming on board that yacht, Miss Eleanor?"

"I certainly do," said Eleanor, her lips firmly set, and an angry gleam in her eyes. "You did exactly the right thing. It was better for us to be worried for a few minutes than to take any chance of spoiling all you'd found out."

"What do you suppose they'll try to do now?" wondered Margery. "Oh, I'd like to find some way to beat them, so that they'd have to stop this altogether."

"They'll go too far, some time," said Eleanor, indignantly. "Mr. Holmes seems to forget there is such a thing as the law, but if he doesn't look out he'll find that all his money won't save him from it. And I think the time is coming very soon. My father has some money, too, and I'm pretty sure he'll spend as much as he needs to to beat these criminals."

"Can't we go away from here to-night, Miss Eleanor?" asked

Dolly. "They said we'd never do that, and it might fool them."

Everyone looked at Dolly in astonishment. It was a strange proposition to come from her, since she usually was the one who wanted to fight if there seemed to be any possibility of success. Now, however, she looked nervous.

"I don't see how we can, Dolly," said Eleanor. "And, really, I don't believe there's any danger here. Mr. Holmes isn't on the yacht, and these men won't do anything until he is there to direct them. I shall telegraph to Mr. Jamieson in the morning, and he will probably come here. He can reach here by noon, and I think we will be all right here until then."

Dolly said nothing more to her, but when she was alone with Bessie she expressed herself more freely.

"I'm afraid of those men," she said, with a shiver. "I think they're far more dangerous than the gypsies were. Didn't you think, from the way they talked, that they would do anything if they thought they would get well paid for it?"

"Yes, but we're warned, Dolly. It isn't as if we didn't have any idea, as they believe, that there is danger here. So I don't think we need to be afraid."

On the beach, between the sea and the tents, the blaze of the camp fire flickered in the darkness, casting an uneven light on the beach. On the yacht all was still and peaceful. One by one her lights had gone out, until only the anchor lights, which she was required by law to show, remained.

"They've gone to sleep on board the yacht," whispered Bessie. "That looks as if they didn't mean to do anything to-night, doesn't it, Dolly?"

"I suppose so, Bessie. But I'm not satisfied."

Neither, wholly, in spite of her reassuring words, was Eleanor. Had there been any way of moving from the camp that night, she would probably have taken it. But there seemed to be nothing for it but to wait there until morning, at least.

"We'll stay here," she said, as good-nights were being exchanged, "but we'll set a guard for the night. Margery, I wish you and Mary King would take the first watch. You'll be relieved at one o'clock. You're not too tired, are you?"

"No, indeed," said both girls.

"I think I ought to take the watch. This is partly on my account," said Bessie.

"Sleep first, and perhaps you can take the second spell, with Dolly," said Eleanor. "You've had a harder day than the rest of us, and you must be tired now."

Bessie and Dolly were, indeed, very tired. The fact that the camp was not to be left unguarded while they slept seemed to reassure Dolly, and she and Bessie were soon sound asleep. Only the noise of the light surf disturbed the intense stillness, and that had a soothing, musical quality that made it far from a disturbance to those who slept.

But that peace was to be rudely shattered before the first watch was over. It was just after midnight when a wild tumult aroused the camp, and Bessie and Dolly, springing to their feet, saw that the beach was as light as day—and that the light did not come from the camp fire. Confused and sleepy as they were, they saw the cause in a moment—the big living tent, in which meals were to be eaten in case of rainy weather, was all ablaze, and the wind that had sprung up during the night was blowing the sparks to the other tents, which caught fire as the girls, frightened and almost panic stricken, rushed out.

For a moment there was no concerted effort, but then Eleanor took command of the situation, and in a moment a line had been formed, and pails full of water from the sea were being handed from one girl to another.

The yacht had sprung into life at the first sign of the fire, and now, as the girls worked, they heard the sound of oars, as boats were hurriedly pushed ashore. In a minute a dozen men had joined them in their fight against the fire, and, thanks to this unexpected aid, one or two of the tents, which had been furthest from the one in which the blaze had started, were saved.

The men from the yacht worked heroically, but their presence and their shouts created a new confusion. And in the midst of it Bessie, a pail of water in her hand, saw a man seize Zara and carry her, struggling, toward a boat. She was just about to cry out when a hand covered her mouth, and the next instant she was lifted in strong arms, carried to the boat, and pushed in.

Then two men sprang aboard, and one held the girls, while the other pulled quickly toward the yacht. They were prisoners!

CHAPTER XV

DOLLY RANSOM MAKES GOOD

"Keep still, and you won't be hurt!" commanded the man who held them. Bessie had no choice in the matter for his hand covered her mouth, and, even had she wished to do so, she could not have cried out.

In a moment, too, looking toward Zara, she saw that she had fainted, and her own predicament was made worse than ever, since the ruffian who held her could now devote all his attention to her. So, utterly helpless, and almost ready to despair, Bessie had to submit to being carried up the little companion ladder that ran to the yacht's deck.

As soon as she was on deck a handkerchief was slipped over her eyes, and, though she could hear the low murmur of voices, and was almost sure that one was that of Mr. Holmes, her arch enemy, she could not be positive. Her one hope now was that Dolly or some one of the others on the beach would have seen her abduction. But, even if they had, what could they do?

"Suppose they did see," poor Bessie thought to herself; "they couldn't do anything. It would take a lot of strong men to come on board this yacht and get us off, and the girls

Jane L. Stewart

wouldn't be able to do anything at all."

She was not left long on the yacht's deck. Almost at once she was carried below, and in a few minutes she found herself in a cabin, where the handkerchief was taken from her eyes. The cabin was a pretty one, but Bessie was in no mood to appreciate that. She hated the sight of its luxury; all she wanted was to be back with the girls on the beach, no matter how great the discomfort after the fire might be.

Zara, who had not yet revived, was brought down after her and laid on a sofa. Then she and Bessie were left alone with the big man who had carried Bessie from the beach. She thought that he was Jeff, the man who had left the two faithless sentinels to watch the path from the cliff. And she noticed, to her surprise, that, though his speech and manners were rough, there was a look about him that was not unkindly.

"Now, see here, sis," he said, gently enough, "we don't aim to treat you badly here. You've run away from home, and that's not right. We're going to see that you get back to them as has the best right to look after you, but we don't want you to be uncomfortable."

"How can I help it?" asked Bessie, indignantly.

"Just you behave yourself and keep quiet, and you'll be all right," said Jeff. Bessie was sure of his identity now. "You'll have this pretty room here to yourselves, and you'll have lots to eat. It'll be better food than you got with that pack of chattering girls, too. We'll up anchor and be off pretty soon, and then you can come up on deck and have a good time. But as long as we're here, why, you'll have to stay below."

Bessie got her first gleam of hope from that speech. If they stayed in Green Cove a little while, there was always the chance that something might happen.

"You see, sis," said Jeff, with a grin, "after a while your folks there will find you're missing, and, like enough, they'll suspicion that we done it; took you off, I mean. 'Twouldn't make no great difference if they did know it," Jeff went on. "But the boss thinks it's just as well if we throw them off a bit—guess he wants to have some fun with them."

"Who is your 'boss'?" asked Bessie, quickly. "I should think you would be ashamed of yourself, treating girls who can't fight back this way! Do you call yourself a man?"

"Easy there, sis!" said Jeff, with a roar of laughter. "You can't make me mad. Orders is orders, you know, and you did wrong when you run away like you did. And I ain't tellin' you who the boss is. What you don't know won't hurt you— and that goes for your friends, too."

He left them alone then, and a faint hope was left behind him. Now that she had the chance, Bessie turned her attention to Zara. There was water in the cabin, and in a few minutes she had revived her chum, and was able to tell her what had happened. Poor Zara seemed to be completely overcome.

"Oh, Bessie, we haven't got a chance this time!" she said. "I'll have to go back and work for Farmer Weeks, and you— will they make you go back to Maw Hoover?"

"Never say die, Zara! As long as the yacht stays in the cove there is a chance that we'll be rescued. That man didn't know it, but he'll never be able to make Miss Eleanor believe we're not on this yacht. Listen—what's that?"

Jane L. Stewart

There was a sound of hasty footsteps outside, and Jeff came in hurriedly. He slipped back a panel at one side of the cabin, and revealed a little closet.

"In there with you—both of you!" he said. "And I'm sorry, but you'll have to be quiet, and there's only one way."

In a trice their hands and feet were bound, and handkerchiefs were stuffed into their mouths. Then they were pushed into the closet and the panel was slipped back into place. They were helpless. Unable to speak, or to beat hands or feet against the thin wood, there was no way in which they could make their presence known. And in a moment they knew the reason for this precaution. For, through the wood of the panel, wafer thin, they heard Miss Eleanor's voice.

"You can't deceive me, sir!" they heard her say. "Those girls must be on this yacht, and I warn you that you had better give them up. Kidnapping is a serious offence in this state."

"You can see for yourself they're not here, ma'am," said Jeff. "And I don't take this kindly at all, ma'am. Why, when I saw the fire in your camp, I went ashore with my men to try to help you—and now you make this charge against us."

"I certainly do!" said Eleanor, with spirit. "I am quite sure that this is the only place where my girls can be, and I mean to have them back. As to the fire, you helped us, it is true. But I am as certain as I can be of anything that you had something to do with starting it before you tried to put it out!"

"There's no use talking to you, ma'am, and I won't try it," said Jeff. "If you're crazy enough to believe anything like that, I could talk all day and you'd still believe it. Here's the yacht—you're welcome to go over her and see for yourself.

You won't find the girls, because they're not aboard. That's a good reason, I guess."

"Then let me see Mr. Holmes."

"There you go again, ma'am! Didn't I tell you on deck that there's no such party aboard, and that I never even heard of him? If you're satisfied now, we'll be glad to have you go ashore, because I want to sail. I've got business down the coast."

"I shall not go ashore until I have found my girls," said Eleanor. There were tears of baffled anger in her voice, and Bessie thrilled with indignant sympathy at the idea that she was within a few feet of her best friend without being able to let her know that she was there.

"Then you'll be put ashore—gently, but firmly, as the books say," said Jeff. "You're dead right, ma'am, kidnappin' is a bad sort of business in this state, and I don't aim to give you a chance to say we carried you off with us against your will. Sail we will—and you'll stay behind. This is my boat, and I've got a right to put off anyone that is trespassin'."

"You brute!" gasped Eleanor. "Don't you dare to touch me!"

"Will you go of your own accord, then?"

"I suppose I must," gasped Eleanor tearfully. "But you shall pay for this, you scoundrel! You're tricking me in some fashion, but you can't deceive me, and you can't keep the truth quiet forever."

Then there was the sound of retreating footsteps, and a few minutes later Bessie and Zara were released by Jeff, who was grinning as if it had been a great joke.

"Well, sis, we're off now!" he said. "Come on! I don't want to be hard on you. Come out here in the passageway, and you can have a look at the shore as we go off."

He led them to the stern, and to the little cabin, in which was a porthole. Looking out, Bessie saw the beach indistinctly. The ruined tents were there, and several of the girls, in bathing suits. And, swimming slowly to the shore she saw a girl in a red cap, which, as she knew, belonged to Dolly. How she longed to be able to call to her! But Jeff was at her side, and she knew that the attempt would be useless, since he was watching her as if he had been a cat and she a mouse.

A bell clanged somewhere below them, and the next moment there was a rumbling sound as the machinery was started. At the same moment there came the grinding of the anchor chains as they were raised. But the yacht did not move! Even after the anchor was up there was no movement except the throbbing of the whole vessel as the engines raced in the hold! Jeff's face grew black, and he turned toward the passage with a scowl.

"What's wrong here?" he shouted, going to the door. At the same moment, seizing her brief chance, Bessie gave a wild scream, and saw, to her delight, that those on shore had heard it. In a moment she was pulled roughly from the porthole, and Jeff, his face savage and all the kindness gone out of it, scowled down at her.

"Keep quiet, you little vixen!" he shouted. "Here, come with me!"

At the foot of some steps that led up to the deck he left the two girls in the care of Larry, one of the two men she had seen the night before.

"Keep them quiet," he commanded, as he sprang up the steps. "What's wrong, Larry; do you know?"

"Something the matter with the propeller. Can't tell what," said Larry.

And above, on the deck, there was a wild rushing about now. Orders were shouted to the engineers below; hoarse answers came back. The engines were stopped and started again. But still the yacht did not move. A grimy engineer came up and stood beside her.

"Propeller's fouled," he said to Jeff. "We'll have to send a man overboard to clear it."

"How long will that take?" roared Jeff.

"Maybe an hour—if we're lucky."

"You're a fine engineer, not to have the boat ready to start!" screamed Jeff, mad with rage. "You'll lose your berth for this!"

"Guess I can get another," replied the engineer calmly. "It's been done on purpose and it's the business of the deck watch to keep the stern clear, not mine."

With frantic haste a man was sent overboard. He dived and found the propeller. Bessie heard his report. The screw was twisted around with rope—knotted and tied so that, even with a knife he would have to make many descents to clear it. Without a diving suit it was impossible for the man to stay under water more than half a minute at a time, and, as it turned out, he was the only man on board who could dive at all.

Jane L. Stewart

Jeff raged in vain. The work of clearing the propeller could not be hastened for all his bellowing, and the precious minutes slipped by while the diver worked. Each time that he came up for rest and air he reported a little more progress, but each time, too, as he grew tired, his period of rest was lengthened, while his time below the water was cut shorter.

And then, when he had reported that two more trips would mend the trouble, there was a sudden bumping of boats against the yacht, on the shoreward side, which had been left without watchers, it seemed, and there was a rush of feet overhead. Bessie cried out in joy, and the next instant a dozen men tumbled down the steps and overpowered Larry.

"Are you Bessie King?" asked their leader. "I've got a search warrant empowering me to search this yacht for you and one Zara Doe and take you ashore."

"We're the ones! Take us!" pleaded Bessie.

And, sobbing with joy, she went up the steps to the deck. There Jeff, furious but powerless in the grip of two men, watched her go over the side and into a small boat in which sat Eleanor, who threw her arms joyously about the recovered captives. Dolly was there, too, and she kissed and hugged Bessie as soon as Eleanor was done.

"The men got here in time from Bay City," said Eleanor. "Thank Heaven! A few minutes more, and they would have been too late. I telephoned as soon as I could, and I knew the district attorney there was a friend of Charlie Jamieson. He came at once with his men."

"The propeller was fouled. That's why they couldn't get away," said Bessie. "Wasn't that lucky?"

Dolly snorted.

"Luck nothing!" she said, perkily. "I swam out with a rope, and they never saw me! I was there, diving up and down, for half an hour. I thought they'd have a lovely time getting it clear when the knots I made had swollen up!"

"Yes, it was Dolly who saved the day," said Eleanor.

"Shall we row you ashore, ma'am, or do you want to see the rest of the fun on board?" asked one of the oarsmen.

"Take us ashore, please. I'll hear all about it later," said Eleanor.

And in five minutes the Camp Fire Girls were reunited.

Jane L. Stewart

Choose from Thousands of 1stWorldLibrary Classics By

A. M. Barnard	Booth Tarkington	Edward Everett Hale
Ada Leverson	Boyd Cable	Edward J. O'Biren
Adolphus William Ward	Bram Stoker	Edward S. Ellis
Aesop	C. Collodi	Edwin L. Arnold
Agatha Christie	C. E. Orr	Eleanor Atkins
Alexander Aaronsohn	C. M. Ingleby	Eleanor Hallowell Abbott
Alexander Kielland	Carolyn Wells	Eliot Gregory
Alexandre Dumas	Catherine Parr Traill	Elizabeth Gaskell
Alfred Gatty	Charles A. Eastman	Elizabeth McCracken
Alfred Ollivant	Charles Amory Beach	Elizabeth Von Arnim
Alice Duer Miller	Charles Dickens	Ellem Key
Alice Turner Curtis	Charles Dudley Warner	Emerson Hough
Alice Dunbar	Charles Farrar Browne	Emilie F. Carlen
Allen Chapman	Charles Ives	Emily Bronte
Alleyne Ireland	Charles Kingsley	Emily Dickinson
Ambrose Bierce	Charles Klein	Enid Bagnold
Amelia E. Barr	Charles Hanson Towne	Enilor Macartney Lane
Amory H. Bradford	Charles Lathrop Pack	Erasmus W. Jones
Andrew Lang	Charles Romyn Dake	Ernie Howard Pie
Andrew McFarland Davis	Charles Whibley	Ethel May Dell
Andy Adams	Charles Willing Beale	Ethel Turner
Angela Brazil	Charlotte M. Braeme	Ethel Watts Mumford
Anna Alice Chapin	Charlotte M. Yonge	Eugene Sue
Anna Sewell	Charlotte Perkins Stetson	Eugenie Foa
Annie Besant	Clair W. Hayes	Eugene Wood
Annie Hamilton Donnell	Clarence Day Jr.	Eustace Hale Ball
Annie Payson Call	Clarence E. Mulford	Evelyn Everett-green
Annie Roe Carr	Clemence Housman	Everard Cotes
Annonaymous	Confucius	F. H. Cheley
Anton Chekhov	Coningsby Dawson	F. J. Cross
Archibald Lee Fletcher	Cornelis DeWitt Wilcox	F. Marion Crawford
Arnold Bennett	Cyril Burleigh	Fannie E. Newberry
Arthur C. Benson	D. H. Lawrence	Federick Austin Ogg
Arthur Conan Doyle	Daniel Defoe	Ferdinand Ossendowski
Arthur M. Winfield	David Garnett	Fergus Hume
Arthur Ransome	Dinah Craik	Florence A. Kilpatrick
Arthur Schnitzler	Don Carlos Janes	Fremont B. Deering
Arthur Train	Donald Keyhoe	Francis Bacon
Atticus	Dorothy Kilner	Francis Darwin
B.H. Baden-Powell	Dougan Clark	Frances Hodgson Burnett
B. M. Bower	Douglas Fairbanks	Frances Parkinson Keyes
B. C. Chatterjee	E. Nesbit	Frank Gee Patchin
Baroness Emmuska Orczy	E. P. Roe	Frank Harris
Baroness Orczy	E. Phillips Oppenheim	Frank Jewett Mather
Basil King	E. S. Brooks	Frank L. Packard
Bayard Taylor	Earl Barnes	Frank V. Webster
Ben Macomber	Edgar Rice Burroughs	Frederic Stewart Isham
Bertha Muzzy Bower	Edith Van Dyne	Frederick Trevor Hill
Bjornstjerne Bjornson	Edith Wharton	Frederick Winslow Taylor

Friedrich Kerst
Friedrich Nietzsche
Fyodor Dostoyevsky
G.A. Henty
G.K. Chesterton
Gabrielle E. Jackson
Garrett P. Serviss
Gaston Leroux
George A. Warren
George Ade
Geroge Bernard Shaw
George Cary Eggleston
George Durston
George Ebers
George Eliot
George Gissing
George MacDonald
George Meredith
George Orwell
George Sylvester Viereck
George Tucker
George W. Cable
George Wharton James
Gertrude Atherton
Gordon Casserly
Grace E. King
Grace Gallatin
Grace Greenwood
Grant Allen
Guillermo A. Sherwell
Gulielma Zollinger
Gustav Flaubert
H. A. Cody
H. B. Irving
H.C. Bailey
H. G. Wells
H. H. Munro
H. Irving Hancock
H. R. Naylor
H. Rider Haggard
H. W. C. Davis
Haldeman Julius
Hall Caine
Hamilton Wright Mabie
Hans Christian Andersen
Harold Avery
Harold McGrath
Harriet Beecher Stowe
Harry Castlemon
Harry Coghill
Harry Houidini

Hayden Carruth
Helent Hunt Jackson
Helen Nicolay
Hendrik Conscience
Hendy David Thoreau
Henri Barbusse
Henrik Ibsen
Henry Adams
Henry Ford
Henry Frost
Henry James
Henry Jones Ford
Henry Seton Merriman
Henry W Longfellow
Herbert A. Giles
Herbert Carter
Herbert N. Casson
Herman Hesse
Hildegard G. Frey
Homer
Honore De Balzac
Horace B. Day
Horace Walpole
Horatio Alger Jr.
Howard Pyle
Howard R. Garis
Hugh Lofting
Hugh Walpole
Humphry Ward
Ian Maclaren
Inez Haynes Gillmore
Irving Bacheller
Isabel Cecilia Williams
Isabel Hornibrook
Israel Abrahams
Ivan Turgenev
J.G.Austin
J. Henri Fabre
J. M. Barrie
J. M. Walsh
J. Macdonald Oxley
J. R. Miller
J. S. Fletcher
J. S. Knowles
J. Storer Clouston
J. W. Duffield
Jack London
Jacob Abbott
James Allen
James Andrews
James Baldwin

James Branch Cabell
James DeMille
James Joyce
James Lane Allen
James Lane Allen
James Oliver Curwood
James Oppenheim
James Otis
James R. Driscoll
Jane Abbott
Jane Austen
Jane L. Stewart
Janet Aldridge
Jens Peter Jacobsen
Jerome K. Jerome
Jessie Graham Flower
John Buchan
John Burroughs
John Cournos
John F. Kennedy
John Gay
John Glasworthy
John Habberton
John Joy Bell
John Kendrick Bangs
John Milton
John Philip Sousa
John Taintor Foote
Jonas Lauritz Idemil Lie
Jonathan Swift
Joseph A. Altsheler
Joseph Carey
Joseph Conrad
Joseph E. Badger Jr
Joseph Hergesheimer
Joseph Jacobs
Jules Vernes
Julian Hawthrone
Julie A Lippmann
Justin Huntly McCarthy
Kakuzo Okakura
Karle Wilson Baker
Kate Chopin
Kenneth Grahame
Kenneth McGaffey
Kate Langley Bosher
Kate Langley Bosher
Katherine Cecil Thurston
Katherine Stokes
L. A. Abbot
L. T. Meade

L. Frank Baum
Latta Griswold
Laura Dent Crane
Laura Lee Hope
Laurence Housman
Lawrence Beasley
Leo Tolstoy
Leonid Andreyev
Lewis Carroll
Lewis Sperry Chafer
Lilian Bell
Lloyd Osbourne
Louis Hughes
Louis Joseph Vance
Louis Tracy
Louisa May Alcott
Lucy Fitch Perkins
Lucy Maud Montgomery
Luther Benson
Lydia Miller Middleton
Lyndon Orr
M. Corvus
M. H. Adams
Margaret E. Sangster
Margret Howth
Margaret Vandercook
Margaret W. Hungerford
Margret Penrose
Maria Edgeworth
Maria Thompson Daviess
Mariano Azuela
Marion Polk Angellotti
Mark Overton
Mark Twain
Mary Austin
Mary Catherine Crowley
Mary Cole
Mary Hastings Bradley
Mary Roberts Rinehart
Mary Rowlandson
M. Wollstonecraft Shelley
Maud Lindsay
Max Beerbohm
Myra Kelly
Nathaniel Hawthrone
Nicolo Machiavelli
O. F. Walton
Oscar Wilde

Owen Johnson
P.G. Wodehouse
Paul and Mabel Thorne
Paul G. Tomlinson
Paul Severing
Percy Brebner
Percy Keese Fitzhugh
Peter B. Kyne
Plato
Quincy Allen
R. Derby Holmes
R. L. Stevenson
R. S. Ball
Rabindranath Tagore
Rahul Alvares
Ralph Bonehill
Ralph Henry Barbour
Ralph Victor
Ralph Waldo Emmerson
Rene Descartes
Ray Cummings
Rex Beach
Rex E. Beach
Richard Harding Davis
Richard Jefferies
Richard Le Gallienne
Robert Barr
Robert Frost
Robert Gordon Anderson
Robert L. Drake
Robert Lansing
Robert Lynd
Robert Michael Ballantyne
Robert W. Chambers
Rosa Nouchette Carey
Rudyard Kipling
Saint Augustine
Samuel B. Allison
Samuel Hopkins Adams
Sarah Bernhardt
Sarah C. Hallowell
Selma Lagerlof
Sherwood Anderson
Sigmund Freud
Standish O'Grady
Stanley Weyman
Stella Benson
Stella M. Francis

Stephen Crane
Stewart Edward White
Stijn Streuvels
Swami Abhedananda
Swami Parmananda
T. S. Ackland
T. S. Arthur
The Princess Der Ling
Thomas A. Janvier
Thomas A Kempis
Thomas Anderton
Thomas Bailey Aldrich
Thomas Bulfinch
Thomas De Quincey
Thomas Dixon
Thomas H. Huxley
Thomas Hardy
Thomas More
Thornton W. Burgess
U. S. Grant
Upton Sinclair
Valentine Williams
Various Authors
Vaughan Kester
Victor Appleton
Victor G. Durham
Victoria Cross
Virginia Woolf
Wadsworth Camp
Walter Camp
Walter Scott
Washington Irving
Wilbur Lawton
Wilkie Collins
Willa Cather
Willard F. Baker
William Dean Howells
William le Queux
W. Makepeace Thackeray
William W. Walter
William Shakespeare
Winston Churchill
Yei Theodora Ozaki
Yogi Ramacharaka
Young E. Allison
Zane Grey

www.ingramcontent.com/pod-product-compliance
Lightning Source LLC
Chambersburg PA
CBHW051832170626
46807CB00003B/1139